Past-into-Present Series

TEXTILES

Hugh Bodey

B T BATSFORD LTD, London & Sydney

First published 1976
© Hugh Bodey 1976

ISBN O 7134 3052 4

Printed by The Anchor Press, Tiptree, Essex
for the Publishers B. T. Batsford Ltd,
4 Fitzhardinge Street London W1H OAH
23 Cross Street Brookvale NSW 2100 Australia

For Ruth and Patrick

Acknowledgment

The Author and Publishers would like to thank the following for their kind permission to reproduce copyright illustrations: Schweiz Landesmuseum, Zurich, for fig 1; *British Farmer and Stockbreeder* for fig 2; The National Museum, Denmark, for fig 5; Verulamium Museum, St Albans, for fig 6; the Mansell Collection for figs 7, 16; the Trustees of the British Museum for fig 9; A.F. Kersting for fig 15; the National Maritime Museum for fig 18; the Science Museum, London, for figs 19, 26; Colne Valley Museum for figs 34, 38, 40; the School of Scottish Studies, University of Edinburgh, for fig 42; ICI Fibres for figs 55, 56; Llew E. Morgan, Swansea, for fig 57; M. Hepworth for fig 39; and Bord Failte, Ireland for fig 59. Figs 3, 20, 35, 36, 48, 58 and 60 are the property of the Author.

Contents

List of Illustrations

1. Introduction

Stone Age cavemen clothed themselves in the skins of sheep and goats. Bronze Age people, who arrived in Britain at intervals between 1900 and 1500 BC, could sew clothes out of woven cloths: a woollen shroud was unearthed during the excavation of a Bronze Age barrow at Rylstone in Yorkshire. It is not possible to say, though, when the art of making cloth came into use in Britain. Wool, cotton and linen had been woven in Asia and the Middle East for a very long time before the Bronze Age started in Britain — pieces of linen woven about 4500 BC have been found in Egypt. It seems certain that information about the processes involved took several thousand years to reach Britain, and that no kind of cloth was woven in the country before 2000 BC. No written

1 A reconstruction of a piece of Stone Age embroidery, based on an excavated remnant from Switzerland. The reconstruction makes it possible to see the kind of stitches used.

2 This Soay sheep on the island of St Kilda is the nearest descendant of the sheep that roamed Britain in prehistoric times. The fleece contains both wool and hair, and can be plucked in the spring. As can be seen, the fleece is made up of several colours.

records were made at that time, of course, so that information can only come from archaeological excavations.

This is no great help, because it is very rare for cloth to survive for long in the ground – the shroud at Rylstone did not perish only because it was in an oak coffin buried in a dry barrow. Wool is even more perishable than cotton and linen, but it was the most common fibre to be woven in Britain. This was because raw cotton would have had to be imported and linen involved very complex processes, whereas wild sheep already lived in Britain. The tools used to make the cloth were not much better than the cloth itself from the point of view of survival in the ground. Spindles and looms were of wood, weaving combs were usually carved out of bone, and only loom and spindle weights were made of anything stronger — stone or broken pottery. These are hard to identify in an excavation, and almost impossible to date accurately on their own. Nothing has come to light so far to prove that cloth of any kind was being made in Britain before 2000 BC, though it is a possibility.

Bronze Age

Information increases with the Bronze Age, and it is possible to give a general idea of the ways of making cloth, and of the kinds of cloth made. Wool seems to have been the only fibre used. This was probably largely because sheep ran wild in the woods that covered most of the country. A few villages like Grimspound on Dartmoor were surrounded with walls high enough to contain sheep though of no defensive value. It is even possible that towards the end of the Bronze Age sheep were being deliberately bred.

The most widespread breed at the time closely resembled the Soay sheep that are now found only on the Scottish island of St Kilda. These are small sheep, and their fleece contains hair as well as wool. They moult early in the summer, and the wool is easy to pluck. Each sheep gives about 500 grams of wool a year. Prehistoric sheep probably had the same range of colours as the Soay sheep. Most of them have a fleece that is chocolate brown but one in three of them is fawn and a few are either black or reddish brown. This variety of colours allowed some patterns to be woven without the need of any dyeing.

Spinning

Leaves, dung and other rubbish had to be taken out of the wool by hand. After that the wool was washed — the roots of soapwort provided sufficient solvent to remove most of the natural grease in the fibres.

The dried wool was then ready for spinning. It was wedged into the fork of a stick, called a distaff, which was tucked under the spinner's arm to serve as a reservoir for the fibres. The spinner drew out the fibres as evenly as possible and knotted them onto the top of a spindle; that was another stick, some 15-20 cm long, and as thick as a pencil. A small stone or piece of pottery was wedged onto the lower end of the spindle, to act both as a weight and a flywheel. It was called a whorl. The art of spinning was to combine two actions at the same time — drawing the fibres out evenly, and twisting them together. The method was to twist the spindle between finger and thumb (like a top) and then let it drop. The weight of the whorl on the spindle drew out the fibres and at the same time kept them twisting. The result was a strong yarn, which was wound

7

onto the spindle every time it reached the ground. It was a slow business but no better way was found until the Middle Ages.

Weaving

Yarn was woven into cloth on a loom. The most common kind of loom at this time was a warp-weighted loom, which could be leaned against the outer wall of the family hut, either inside or out. It was made of two strong side poles, resting on the ground and leaning back against the wall. These were held apart by rails at top and bottom. Lengths of yarn were pinned to the top rail, and hung down almost to the ground. These were the warp threads which would

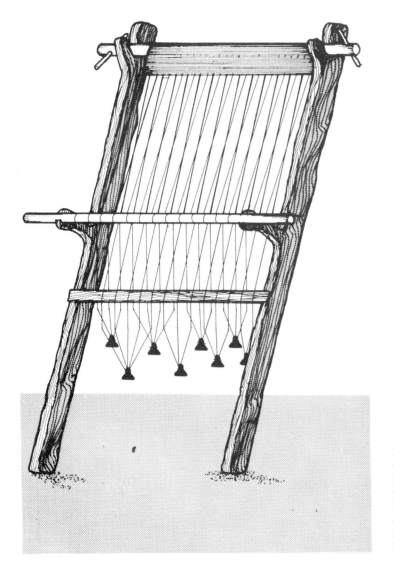

3 An artist's reconstruction of a warp-weighted loom in diagram form. The warp pole is shown pulled forward onto the rests, so drawing some warp threads in front of others. These were released when the pole was replaced against the frame, changing the shed.

give the finished cloth its strength. Alternate threads were pulled forward to hang in front of the bottom rail, leaving the others hanging vertically. These back threads were individually attached to a moveable pole with loops of cord; the pole could be pulled forward onto rests projecting from the frame of the loom, and when this was done the rear yarns passed between the others until they were in front. The yarn was gathered into bundles, and each bundle weighted with stones, pottery or metal rings. It took longer to make the loom ready for use than it did to weave a piece of cloth, but when all this was done, the loom was ready for weaving.

The weaver passed a hank of wool through the gap between the threads at the front and those hanging straight down at the back. (This gap is called the shed.) One thread, known as the weft thread, was left in the shed when the weaver took the hank out the other side, and this was then pushed up tightly against the top rail with a comb of wood or bone. The first weft thread had been woven. The weaver pulled the moveable bar onto the rests, pulling the rear fibres forward. This crossed the two sets of warp threads, and locked the weft in place. The hank of weft was passed back through the shed, the thread pushed up tightly, and the rod released for the third weft to be put in. Clearly weaving was even slower than spinning, and required considerable concentration and endurance. The weaver continued until he had worked down as far as the rod. He could go no further, so cut that piece of cloth out of the loom and had to start warping the loom for the next one. (Looms could have had a roller, enabling longer pieces to be woven.)

It is possible that another kind of loom was also used in the Bronze Age. This is known as a two-beam loom. It had the same frame as the other loom but there were no weights. Instead, warp threads were hung from the horizontal beam at the top, and fastened to another at the bottom to keep them straight. This made it quicker to put the warp into the loom but much harder to weave. Since it was impossible to cross the warp threads to change the shed, the process of weaving was nearer to darning. The cloth was not as well-made, was less warm and would not have lasted as long.

Patterns

Much of the cloth made at this time was no doubt plain weave, that is each weft thread simply going over one warp and under the next. This does not make a pattern in the cloth, but it is the easiest to weave and as warm as any other. Cloth fragments found in excavations show that a variety of twill patterns were also woven. These have a pattern running diagonally across the cloth, and can be made even more attractive by using one colour for the warp and another for the weft. The warp-weighted loom could be easily adapted to make such patterns.

Apart from a final wash to remove any remaining grease and dirt, it would

4 Diagrams to show the formation of plain weave cloth (*left*) and twill (*right*). The white threads are the warp.

seem that the cloth was used in its natural state. No evidence of dyeing equipment has so far been found. This does not prove that the early weavers could not dye cloth — much could be done in an earthenware bowl or a wooden bucket. Other finishing processes that were common in later centuries may also have been used, but a lack of any surviving tools makes it impossible to say that they were. There were certainly no factories and probably no workshops; each family made as much cloth as it needed and no more. There was no export trade in cloth at this time, and it is unlikely that even neighbouring villages bought much from one another.

Iron Age

About 500 BC small groups of farmers began to arrive in southern England from the mainland of Europe. They brought with them a knowledge of smelting and working iron, and because of this the term Iron Age is used to describe the next six centuries. This does not mean that people promptly stopped using bronze. Instead, the two groups of people tended to stay in their own villages, fighting each other if they came too close but more often trading with each other and with communities as far away as the Mediterranean as well. In addition to their skill with iron, it seems that the newcomers also had some knowledge of making linen, and they certainly found ways of improving the quality of native wool, as the next chapter will show. British manufacturers began exporting cloth in the last century BC, and exports of textiles will be a recurring theme in this book.

The word 'textiles' is a group name for all woven materials. At first these were all made from natural fibres available locally, such as wool and the flax used to make linen. In later centuries, the longer wool fibres were combed out of the rest to make worsted cloth, and new fibres like cotton and jute were imported and manufactured into quite different cloths. Man-made synthetic fibres began to be widely used in the twentieth century and, since they were also woven, they were added to the widening range of textiles. Problems of definition came with the development of non-woven cloths in the 1960s. These have generally been referred to as textiles because they are more like cloth than anything else and are used for similar purposes.

This book is concerned with the development of textiles, and the machines and processes designed to make them. It is very much a human story. Cloth is only made to fulfil a need, which is usually to clothe somebody. Changes in fashion have been present since Roman times at least. Fashion depends on the colours that are available to dye cloth and on the designs that can be made with different machines and fibres. The other side of the textile story is that the manufacture of cloth is work for someone, and conditions of work have changed greatly over the centuries.

2. Celts and Romans

The Iron Age people are sometimes referred to as Britons or as Celts. Later invaders continually pushed them north and west, so that today their descendants live mainly in Scotland, the far north of England, Wales and Cornwall, though other nationalities have also moved into these areas from time to time. By 400 BC Celtic villages were thinly scattered throughout southern England, where forests could be cleared and the ground was fertile. Sheep and other animals roamed in the woods and fed themselves, and the quality and quantity of wool was no better than it had been for centuries.

Celtic Technology

The Bronze Age people were essentially farmers: though they could make the tools and other goods they needed for daily life, they seem to have been more interested in mastering the business of farming than anything else. The Celts also had to spend most of their time farming. Indeed this was the case right up to the eighteenth century, because people had not discovered the techniques which would make it possible for a family to grow more than it needed for itself. As a result there was no surplus to feed those who might otherwise have been employed in some industrial activity. Despite this, however, it seems that the Celts had a greater interest in technical matters than the Bronze Age people, and that they were keen to develop industries as far as they could within the limitations imposed by the time-consuming farms. Mining for lead, copper, tin and iron was developed and extended to many parts of Britain, and the goods made with these metals were not only useful but in some cases very attractive. Brooches for fastening cloaks, to take one example, were made into many imaginative shapes, and often decorated with bright enamels.

The Celts' metal-working skills are known because many of their tools and manufactured goods have survived. Mines too have left their mark. Much less is known about textiles because cloth and the tools used to make it are perishable. Such evidence as there is suggests that the Celts brought the same

5 (*Opposite*) A long kilt and cloak, made from plain weave woollen cloth by Iron Age craftsmen. It was found in Denmark.

13

level of enthusiastic improvement to cloth production as they did to other industries.

Better Wool

The first essential was to improve the quality of the raw wool, since nothing could be done without that. About 200 BC, new breeds of sheep were imported into Britain from Gaul (France) and other parts of Europe. These seem to have produced curly white wool rather than the hairy multi-coloured wool of the wild sheep. There are signs that these sheep were bred on farms in Suffolk, Cambridgeshire and on the South Downs, which suggests that the farmers concerned knew the value of the wool, and were taking some trouble to produce more of it.

Other pieces of the archaeological jigsaw add to the feeling that Celtic cloth-makers were keen to widen the range of goods they made, and information from the writings of Roman officials and army officers supplements finds from excavations. The Romans began the serious conquest of Britain in AD 43, and quickly colonized south-east England. They spread out from there towards the west, taking over the lucrative lead mines in the Mendip Hills in Somerset by 49, and then moved steadily northwards. Main garrison towns were built at Gloucester, Chester and York, and most English tribes were having to pay taxes to the Romans by the end of the first century. The Romans had been attracted to Britain mainly by the wealth of metal ores in the ground and the known skills of British craftsmen. They were less interested in textiles, regarding British cloth as most unfashionable, though they took plenty of plain weave woollen cloth in taxation towards clothing the troops quartered in Britain. The Romans added few new ideas to the production techiques used in the country, and their influence on cloth design only extended to weavers in those towns where there were many Roman customers. The information available about Roman Britain can therefore be taken to describe the Celtic ways of making and designing cloth, and the few Roman innovations can be left until later in the chapter.

Production methods continued much the same as in Bronze Age times. The raw wool was washed, pulled out into thick strands (called rovings) and spun with a drop spindle. These spindles were expensive. In the fourth century AD they cost twelve pence each, which was the same as a dozen eggs or a pound of pork. The warp-weighted loom was preferred for weaving, because of the complex patterns that could be woven on it. By this time the weaving combs were made of wood, which lasted longer.

Dyeing and Finishing

The main improvements during this period were in the finishing of the cloth after it was taken out of the loom. Dyeing, for example, was done by skilled craftsmen who built workshops onto their homes to hold the equipment for their work. The most expensive item was a boiler, which was built of stone and lined with a thin copper vat. Wood, or coal if it could be obtained locally, was used to fire the boiler, so there was a fuel store near the workshop as well.

Most dyes will not dye cloth by themselves. Instead, the cloth has first to absorb a chemical which reacts with the dye to fix it in the cloth. The chemical is called a mordant. Alum and iron salts were used as mordants in Roman times, and to ensure that the mordant had been absorbed into the cloth and would not wash out afterwards, the cloth was boiled up in a solution containing one of them. The dyes were obtained from plants, such as lichens, woad, madder and whortleberry, and from some shells — whelks were often used. The cloth was again boiled in whichever dye was being used, and over a period of several hours the cloth took on a new colour. Wool that was to be used in patterned cloths was dyed before it was spun and woven.

The other group of finishing processes was often done in a separate workshop and by other craftsmen. Their task was to change the cloth from a loose fabric something like sacking into a warm and hard-wearing cloth. The first stage was fulling, which partially broke down the yarn and made the fibres felt together on both sides of the cloth. To do this, the cloth was put into a shallow bath and soapy water was added. The 'soap' came from soapwort, or fuller's earth, which was a mild detergent that could be dug from the ground as clay in several parts of Britain. The solvent in the water helped the fibres to cling together, but the fuller had to make this happen by trampling on the cloth for hours at a time. The continuous pounding felted the fibres together, which made the cloth stronger and warmer. (The men who did this were often called walkers, which became quite a common surname much later, in the Middle Ages.)

Woollen cloth shrinks when it is washed. After fulling, the fuller stretched it back again and hung it out to dry on a frame covered in sharp nails, called tenter-hooks, to hold the cloth in shape. The cloth now looked like a worn blanket, and had to be improved before it was fit to sell. The fuller went over the cloth with teazles, whose prickles raised up the fibres and made the cloth very woolly — it now resembled a new blanket. Finally, large cropping shears were used to cut away all the unwanted fibres, leaving a smooth piece of cloth that was ready to wear. The better quality cloths were fulled for two days, and might be raised and cropped three or four times, but most cloths were only done once. Considerable skill and experience were needed to dye and finish cloth, and dyers and fullers were almost full-time industrial workers. But even they downed tools to join the farmers at seedtime, haymaking and harvest.

Most of the population wore plain cloths, which each family wove for itself. These were plain-weave fabrics, and the natural colour of the wool. The weavers could produce a wide variety of types and patterns of cloth for those

15

who could afford them. Tartans were being woven by 55 BC, for instance, as well as twills and checks. (The Romans liked twill patterns but thought checks were effeminate.) Striped cloths were woven as were herringbone stripes, which required considerable skill and concentration from the weaver.

Exports

Some of the cloths made in Britain were exported. They had been before the Roman conquest, and Roman merchants extended the export trade by buying cloth and sending it to all parts of the Empire. British cloths were liked because of their good quality, and in the fourth century rugs from Scotland fetched more money than any others. The Romans brought with them the technique of combing wool, to separate short fibres from long. The long fibres were spun into yarn that was woven into showerproof capes and cloaks, which were also popular in other countries. Some areas specialized in producing woollen cloth.

6 Some fragments of a woollen shroud used to bury an infant in St Albans in the third century. Look at the weave of the cloth — the pattern made by warp and weft threads.

The lake villages of Meare and Glastonbury in Somerset, for example, were able to buy as much wool as they could use from flock masters grazing sheep on the surrounding hills, and sold cloth to other villages and to merchants for export.

The Roman occupation increased the demand for woollen cloth. The troops quartered in Britain had to be clothed, as had the growing number of administrators and government officials. The civilians bought their own cloth but the troops were supplied with theirs. At first this was taken from weavers as part of taxation, or as tribute from newly conquered tribes. This, however, was not enough, and other ways had to be found of producing large quantities of cheap cloth. A government weaving factory was set up at Winchester in the third century, where many weavers were kept at work under close supervision to produce cloth as quickly as possible. Outdated villas were taken over for some of the other trades — fulling was carried out on a large scale at villas in Chedworth, Titsey and Darenth, and one at Great Chesterford was used for cropping. A dyeworks was set up at Silchester. All this activity was connected with producing cloth for the troops, and it did not add anything to exports. The quality of the cloth produced in this way was what could be expected of mass-produced goods.

Linen
The works at Winchester also spun linen cloth, though this was not new to Britain either — it had been manufactured here since about 150 BC. It was made from flax, a plant midway between a coarse grass and thin reed, which grew wild in many parts of Britain. After harvesting, the flax had to stand in water for some weeks to rot a little, in order to loosen the fibres. Then it was combed to remove short and coarse fibres (a process called 'hackling' in later centuries). The remaining fibres were long and silky, and women spun them with a drop spindle in the same way as wool. The yarn could be spun much finer than wool, and it was this fine yarn that was woven into linen. (The thick yarns were also spun, and used to weave canvas.) Linen could be woven in various patterns and dyed like wool, but no fulling or cropping was needed. The main attractions of the cloth were that it was thin and smooth, and could be bleached much whiter than wool.

The more complicated production processes made linen expensive, and only a few people could afford it. Chief among these were the Celtic priests, the Druids, who wore white linen robes for religious ceremonies and sometimes for their daily dress. The Romans could also afford to buy linen, and this encouraged more weavers to make it. The wives and daughters of Roman officials particularly liked to wear linen in preference to wool, and it was used too for sheets, tablecloths and napkins, and for towels at the baths. Left to themselves, the Celts would not have bothered to make linen for any of these purposes, but the fact that their wealthy customers used it encouraged them to

17

improve the quality of their cloth and to try new patterns and colours. York was noted for the fine quality of linen made in the area, and no doubt this was partly because Roman customers expected, and would pay for, good quality work.

Linen was also being exported by the fourth century, though the quantities involved were only a fraction of the wool trade.

The Romans began to withdraw their troops from Britain in the fourth century AD, and the last left in 410. It is clear that at that time linen was being woven in many parts of Britain for sale to Roman officials and merchants. Perhaps British tribal chiefs, and their families even more, were also beginning to prefer linen to wool — certainly those who liked to imitate Roman ways did so.

The production of linen, however, was on a small scale compared to the output of woollen cloth. This was made in every town and village, almost by every family, throughout Britain. Most families had to be self-supporting in cloth as with growing food, and could not afford to buy it from anyone else. Some villages deliberately produced a surplus for sale to wealthier customers

and overseas merchants, and the larger villages made enough cloth to find work for specialist dyers, fullers and croppers.

The departure of the Romans did not make an overwhelming difference to the textile workers. There were fewer wealthy customers, which affected the linen producers more than others, but the withdrawal of troops and officials was spread over a long period and allowed time for new customers to be found. Some Romans stayed in Britain, and the use of linen by the native population had also grown. As for the woollen manufacturers, they were hardly affected at all by the Romans going. Exports continued, but the bulk of the cloth made in Britain had always been used in the country, and people still had to be clothed. This reliance on a market for woollen cloth within Britain was to be a permanent feature of the industry, and to stand it in good stead when trade was difficult.

7 This Roman shop sold cloth for togas and cloaks, embroidered belts and cushions. All of these were among the variety of textile goods exported from Britain in Roman times.

3. Linen versus Wool

The centuries that passed between the departure of the last Roman troops in 410 and the arrival of the first Normans in 1066 are known as the Dark Ages. It is the historians who are in the dark. Few written records survive from this time, and very few of those that have refer to industry or work. Archaeologists and historians have been busy in recent years trying to piece together a picture of life in these six centuries, but there is still much to discover.

Invaders

The overriding pattern of this time is one of repeated invasion. The Romans had had to deal with raiders from Saxony in the fourth century, and had succeeded in repulsing them. Without Roman protection, the Celts were no match against invaders who were desperate to find somewhere to live, and boatloads of Saxons, Jutes and Angles began to arrive in England from about 450 onwards. The modern names of Sussex, Middlesex and Essex are evidence of the areas abandoned to the Saxons, and a much larger area covering most of southern England became known as Wessex. East Anglia indicates the land the Angles seized, and in 800 there was a Middle Anglia as well. The native Celts retreated into the hilly areas of the north and west — they had always preferred hill top villages and were better able to defend them.

Viking raids began in 786 and were often bloodthirsty visits. The Vikings came from Norway and Denmark, which were becoming overcrowded, and in the ninth century the raids for booty began to turn into conquest; many coastal areas in all parts of Britain were colonized. The most populated colony was the Danelaw, which from 865 took in much of eastern England. By the year 1000, there were many separate kingdoms within Britain, as well as colonies ruled from other countries. This in turn meant that there were several different languages and many dialects, different coinages and customs, and very little in common between the various regions.

It might seem that manufacturing and trade could hardly survive such a period of drastic change. The invasions and conquests were spread out over five centuries, though, and that is a very long time. In addition, the numbers of people involved were small — Britain was under-populated even in 1000 AD,

8 Like a continuous cartoon strip, the Bayeux Tapestry illustrates not only the heat of battle but the patience and skill of Saxon embroidresses in the eleventh century.

and there was plenty of space for all the invaders to settle. Fighting clearly took place at times, and there were some major pitched battles, particularly when Alfred was king of Wessex between 871 and 899. But for most of the population there were long spells of peace and even stability. This was inevitable — the farming methods used at the time could not feed large permanent armies, and fighting was therefore strictly rationed.

Work Continues

What then, was the fate of the textile trades during this long time? In the first place, people had to be clothed, and there is plenty of evidence to show that

21

families continued to spin woollen yarn and weave cloth throughout this period. Production must have been disrupted if ever the fighting came near but this did not happen repeatedly except in a few unlucky coastal villages.

Woollen cloth production did not stop at just clothing the native population. Cloth was being exported to Europe in the mid-eighth century, and this trade continued into the eleventh century. It is possible that woollens had been exported continuously since Roman times but the lack of information means that there is no proof of this. On the other hand, in the third and fourth centuries, weavers had been used to producing enough cloth for Roman customers and some for export in addition, and it would seem probable that they would have found alternative customers after the Romans left. It is known that woad and madder were being deliberately cultivated in the eighth century (rather than growing wild), to give dyes, and teazles for raising the cloth before cropping. All this suggests that the woollen industry, at any rate, was continuing to produce more cloth than was needed for home consumption in Britain, and that merchants were able to sell the rest. It is probable that most of the cloth was made in people's homes in much the same way as in Iron Age times, and that the cloth was coarse but warm.

A site excavated at Upton in Northamptonshire shows that more organized ways of production were also being used, if only in a few places. The Saxons had built a weaving shed there, 90 metres long and 54 metres wide — at least twice the size of any ordinary cottage at the time. Two warp-weighted looms had been in use, and there were racks for pottery weights on the walls. The building was the home of the weavers but they would have used more yarn than their families could have spun. They may have bought yarn from neighbouring families, or perhaps they put their own wool out to other people to spin. This weaving shed can hardly be called a factory, and yet it does show that there was sufficient demand for woollen cloth to make it worth someone's while to build so large a workshop. It would have been necessary for the weavers to work full-time at the looms to justify the cost of building the shed.

Linen

An ancient Welsh law, dating from about the seventh century, throws some light on changes in fashion. The law stated that household officers were to be given cloth for new clothes three times a year — the king provided the woollen cloth and the queen gave linen. The king probably bought his cloth from weavers around the kingdom, but the queen and her ladies may well have woven the linen themselves. Most clothing was made of wool, and linen was reserved mainly for decoration. It was an expensive material and was only made in small quantities, mostly by ladies of the nobility who were allowed little else to do to while away the time. By the seventh century, linen was being woven in many different patterns, using a variety of colours, and the fineness of linen thread made it a favourite for embroidery.

Three centuries later, linen was still a luxury fabric, but it was being made in greater quantities. Those who could afford it preferred it for underclothes because it was more healthy than wool. It was also more comfortable — wearing a woollen shirt was a common penance in the monasteries. Noble ladies wore loose, flowing linen robes, with deep patterned borders either woven or embroidered. The manufacture of linen must by this time have become quite an industry, and flax was grown in many parts of Britain where conditions were suitable, such as the vale of Yorkshire, Somerset, Wiltshire and many of the southern counties.

By 1066, because of the Danish conquest of eastern England, the amount of flax grown had declined — the land was used for growing food instead. The linen made from British flax was now regarded as coarse, and much finer linen was imported from Flanders. The lower price of linen brought it within the reach of a large number of people, and linen underclothes were common. The industry had clearly developed from the handmade fabric of the Welsh court to reach a stage at which many people were spinning and weaving linen in those areas where flax was readily available.

One side of the linen industry remained the work of noble ladies — embroidery. Saxon women were famed for their skill at this, and demonstrated it in sewing the Bayeux Tapestry. This splendid work, 50 cms high and about 75 metres long, embroidered at the command of the Norman Queen Matilda, records the preparations for the Norman invasion, and the battle that defeated the women who embroidered it.

The Norman Conquest

The Normans were more thorough at keeping records than the Celts and Saxons, so with the conquest a more detailed picture of economic life emerges. Many forest areas were cleared by the new owners of lands confiscated from the Saxons, and flocks of sheep grew larger on the new pastures. Sheep were useful animals to keep — they manured the land, could be sheared every year and provided meat at the end. The output of wool therefore increased in the eleventh century. The population also increased slowly, and naturally had to be clothed. Clearly there was going to be a steady demand for as much woollen cloth as could be made, which would encourage new production methods. Flax, however, could only be grown at the expense of some other crop, and its higher cost of manufacture was bound to make it a fabric that held appeal only for those who could afford it. The exception to this was the coarse form of linen, canvas, which was needed to make sails for the growing number of ships after Alfred had encouraged shipbuilders to copy the Viking longship and forget about coracles. There were fewer ships than sheep, though, and the future lay with developing the wool they produced.

23

4. The Woolsack

The production of fibres and manufacture of fabrics was by far the most important group of industries in Britain during the period of this chapter, 1100-1600. Some kind of cloth was made in every county of Britain, in many cases more than one kind, and the export of wool and woollen cloth provided three-quarters of the country's customs revenue. Woollen cloth was produced in much greater quantities than any other, and must therefore dominate this chapter.

The word 'woollen' has to serve several meanings, and has had to since the Middle Ages. It can mean any kind of cloth made of wool fibres, as distinct from cotton, silk or linen. More narrowly, it can mean cloth made from yarn spun out of carded wool, as against worsted cloth which is made from combed wool. Unfortunately it is impossible to avoid the problem of this double meaning since there is no other word that can be used.

Wool Supply

Several breeds of sheep were at large in the country by 1100, some running wild and others properly shepherded. The quality of their wool was mostly good, particularly that of the Herefordshire and Cotswold breeds. (Later in the Middle Ages 'Cotswold' was almost a brand name for good quality wool in Europe.) Most of the wool available in Britain in 1100 was needed to clothe the population, although a little was exported as wool or cloth.

The arrival of Cistercian monks in the twelfth century was the start of a rapid increase in the number and size of flocks of sheep, and therefore in the output of wool. The Cistercians deliberately chose wild and remote sites for their monasteries, and were given large areas of useless moorland. (Fountains Abbey owned a million acres of Yorkshire by the year 1500.) The monks were skilled sheep breeders before they came to Britain, and they developed the moors for sheep pasture. This took time, of course, but over the years the wool available from the monasteries became considerable — Fountains Abbey sold 27,600 lbs (12,500 kilos) in one year, 1315, and still kept enough to make cloth for themselves and their workers. The Cistercians were not the only monastic order dealing in wool; it was also a major source of income for the

9 A master dyer and his apprentice, from a fifteenth-century manuscript. The copper vat is heated, and the cloth has to be stirred so that it takes the dye evenly. White cloth is waiting on the left to be dyed.

Gilbertine, Augustinian, Benedictine and some smaller orders, and for any monastery in the sheep rearing district, which stretched from Yorkshire through the west Midlands into the Cotswolds. The monks used the money from the sale of wool to build the gracious buildings that still retain their magnificence even in ruin, and for local charitable work.

The monasteries were soon joined by landowners, who began to copy the monks' methods in the thirteenth century. Their share of the market increased steadily throughout the Middle Ages, and they became the main suppliers of wool after the monasteries were closed in the 1530s and their lands given away or sold. One such sixteenth-century sheep rearer was Sir Henry Fermor of East Barsham in Norfolk, who had 15,500 sheep split into twenty flocks.

Producing wool was very profitable for men like him, whose estates were large enough to keep so many sheep. This tempted many landowners to pull down whole villages on their land and convert arable land into sheep pasture, dividing the vast open fields into smaller enclosures. These village clearances mostly took place between 1450 and 1550, in the corn growing counties of Leicestershire, Oxfordshire and particularly Northamptonshire, where one village in eight was pulled down. Wool fetched a higher price than wheat. Some landowners offered their tenants land elsewhere or bought them out; the more unscrupulous evicted the tenants and pulled the houses down in front of them, leaving them to find work and a home where they could. Enclosing the open fields and converting the land to pasture was made illegal in 1488, but most of it had already been done by then, and some was done later regardless of the law. The Prior of Bicester (for churchmen could be as greedy as any) had 200 acres in the Oxfordshire village of Wretchwick, and also five houses with thirty acres to each. Commissioners reported about him:

> He held this land on the second of March 1489 when those houses were laid waste and thrown down, and lands formerly used for arable he turned over to pasture for animals, so that three ploughs are now out of use there, and eighteen people who used to work on that land . . . have gone away to take to the roads in their misery.

By 1550, the demand for wool was declining, while the population was growing and needed more wheat. This achieved what the law had failed to do and brought to an end the pulling down of villages and enclosing of fields.

The largest group of sheep keepers were the villagers in every county, though less is known about them. It would seem that some kept only two or three sheep, though a few in Leicestershire in the sixteenth century had as many as thirty. An average of eight or ten might be a reasonable guess. No precise details exist of the wool produced by peasants, because it was never sold. Instead it was all used to make cloth for the family, and any surplus was sold as cloth. This surplus was slight, and the wool produced for domestic needs will have to be ignored for the time being, despite its volume.

Wool Exports

The monks' and landowners' wool, on the other hand, was produced for sale. The monks sold most of theirs abroad — the load referred to earlier which Fountains Abbey sold in 1315 was bought by merchants from Florence, who signed contracts for several years ahead to take all that was available. Most of the monasteries sold their wool to overseas buyers in this way in the thirteenth century, aided by their links with monasteries throughout Europe. The landowners had no such links and sold their wool to merchants in Britain, who set about exporting it to the main wool markets in Europe. From 1313, the export trade was controlled by the Merchants of the Staple, who laid down regulations as to which ports could be used, how much wool was to be in each pack and so forth. In 1331, for example, Norwich was made the staple port for all wool exported to Flanders from East Anglia, and other districts had their own ports. Calais, a British possession from 1347 to 1558, was frequently the only town through which British wool could pass on its way to the Flemish wool markets. A system of staple ports made the work of the customs officers much easier, though a certain amount of wool was smuggled out of Britain to avoid the heavy duties.

The parliament that met at Oxford in 1258 decided that the wool should be worked up in England instead of being sold to foreigners. Little came of that decision until Edward III (1327-77) realized that he could ask far more in taxes if the raw wool was made into cloth and that exported instead. He banned imports of cloth made abroad, and offered privileges to tempt immigrants from Holland and Flanders, who could bring with them some of the secrets of weaving, dyeing and finishing which made Flemish cloth so much better than British. A number of immigrants came, settling in Norwich, Worstead and other towns in East Anglia and Lincolnshire. Edward III's actions trebled the amount of cloth exported between 1355 and 1395, and the export of raw wool began to decline. The Merchant Adventurers Company was formed in London in 1486, with the same powers over the export of cloth that the staple merchants had over wool.

Woollen cloth was made in every county. It had to be, because every village had to produce all the cloth it needed. Some villages had one man who did all the weaving — one who was not fit enough to farm, perhaps — while in others every family produced its own during the winter. The growing number of cloths for export, however, were increasingly drawn from three main areas. The largest was the West Country, where high quality broadcloths were made in Gloucestershire, Somerset, Wiltshire and Devon. Broadcloths were made of the best wool, and were popular throughout Europe despite their high price. Another principal area for exports was West Yorkshire, where narrow cloths were made from the poorer wools available from neighbouring counties. These were cheap but durable cloths, which sold in great numbers to mid-European countries. The third area was East Anglia, where some broadcloths were made. The Dutch workers had brought with them patterns of new fabrics using worsted yarn which, though made of wool fibres, was combed instead of carded. The worsted cloths were expensive but sold well. In addition to these

27

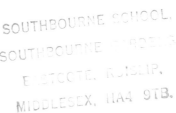

main areas, cloths were exported from Wales, the Lake District, Scotland, Lancashire — in fact from just about everywhere that cloth was made.

New Machines

Edward III would have made little progress in encouraging more cloth to be made if manufacturers had still been dependent on the drop spindle, the warp-weighted loom and men walking the cloth to full it. However, several new machines had been developed which between them made possible the rapid increase in cloth production.

At some time before 1100 spinners had learned that they could make a better thread if the wool was carded first. The purpose of carding was to break open the locks of wool, and leave the fibres roughly parallel when they were taken off the cards. These were made of teazle heads, fixed to a wooden handle. Carded fibres could be drawn out more evenly from the distaff. After 1300 the cards were made of brass wire staples, which made it easier to remove the wool, and spinners' children of nine and ten carded all the wool used from then until machines were developed to do the work in the eighteenth century.

The first spinning wheel came into use in the fourteenth century. This was the great wheel, which gave the spinner more control over drawing out the fibres and therefore made a more even yarn. The great wheel was only slightly

10 The great wheel being used for spinning. The child on the floor has been set to card wool by hand. Each board in her hand was covered with hundreds of wire staples, bent towards the handle. The child pulled these away from each other to separate the wool fibres. The fibres were removed by pushing the cards towards the handles, which rolled the fibres into a sliver for the mother to spin.

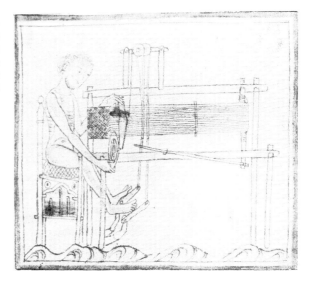

11 A simple form of frame loom. The warp threads unwind from the roller on the right, and pass through healds suspended from the pulleys. Operated by pedals, these create the shed through which the weaver can pass the shuttle.

faster than a drop spindle, and spinning 7 lbs (3 kilos) of wool was a full week's work. The drop spindle was preferred by many people and was still in use in the eighteenth century. A more sophisticated spinning wheel, called the Saxony or Scots wheel, came into Britain about 1480. It was worked by a treadle, at least in the sixteenth century, which left the spinner with both hands free to regulate the flow of fibres and even out any lumps. The Saxony wheel was best at spinning yarns from long fibres, such as linen and worsted, and although it was sometimes used for woollen yarn this was not usual because of its high cost compared with the great wheel.

Another improvement was the frame loom, which came into use about the end of the fourteenth century. This was a dramatic advance over the warp-weighted loom. In place of the fixed length warps, the warp threads were unwound from a roller and could be of any length, though in practice they were usually somewhere between 10 and 25 metres depending on the kind of cloth. Each warp thread passed through the eye of a heald, and healds could be raised or lowered by treadles to change the gap for the weft. This too was altered, for in place of an untidy hank a shuttle was used, which unwound the weft thread evenly. Broadcloths were woven by a weaver and an apprentice, who passed the shuttle from one to the other, though the weaver of a narrow cloth could reach through the shed for himself. To summarize the advantages of the frame loom — it made longer pieces, it was quicker and more convenient, particularly for weaving patterned cloth, and it made better quality cloth. This machine more than any other made possible the great increase in cloth production ordered by Edward III.

One other innovation had improved the quality of fulling since the twelfth century: fulling stocks. These were heavy hammers which pummelled the cloth

12 This medieval illustration shows a mother spinning, with her children at her knee. Slivers of carded wool were tied to the distaff tucked under her left arm, and she drew the fibres out with her left hand. She spun the spindle with her right hand, and then let it fall.

13 (*Opposite*) The woman in the lower picture is preparing a warp. She is drawing a dozen threads at a time from the racks of bobbins, and winding them round the pegs on the warping frame. Warp threads had to be of the same length and an even tension. The monkey is reeling off yarn from a spindle.

in soapy water. They were worked in pairs, and were so heavy that they had to be driven by water power, but their greater weight meant that the fulling was more thorough. The need for water power caused fulling mills to be set up in new areas, as will be seen later in this chapter.

Dyeing

One aspect of cloth production that saw little improvement was dyeing. Flanders was so much the home of good dyeing that British dyers seemed to despair of competing throughout the Middle Ages. Hardly any potash was made or alum mined for mordants, though both could have been done quite easily. It was the same with the plants from which dyes were obtained — woad, madder

and others could be grown in this country, but the limitations of open field farming and a general lack of interest meant that hardly any was. Instead, most cloth that was exported went in the natural state to Flanders, to be dyed and finished there. Some of it was later bought back at a higher price. Even the dyes that were used for cloth finished in Britain were mostly imported, usually again from Flanders. (This reliance on imported dyestuffs lasted until the 1920s.) The use of homegrown alder to dye knitted stockings black in the sixteenth century was a rare example of local products being used.

By 1400, manufacturers had the tools to spin, weave and full the cloth better than ever before, and to a higher standard than craftsmen in many other countries to judge from the success of the exporting merchants, but most of the cloth was exported 'in the white' to be dyed and finished in Flanders. The rapid growth of cloth manufacturing in the fourteenth century made it the country's largest single industry (farming excepted); it employed more people than any other, and was carried on in every county. Its wealth can still be seen in the churches and manor houses built by the merchant-manufacturers in the South West and East Anglia, by the bridges 'built on wool' (on the profits of the trade) and in the memorial brasses to be found in many churches. Most other industries that developed at all in the Middle Ages did so in response to the needs of the woollen manufacturers.

14 Bleaching was a community project in the Middle Ages. The cloth was boiled, hammered with heavy mallets, sprinkled with sour milk and laid out to bleach in the sun. It had to be washed and dried before it was fit to use.

Guilds

The manufacture of cloth for sale (as opposed to making it to clothe the family) was centred in the main towns in the thirteenth and fourteenth centuries, such as London, Bristol and Winchester. In Yorkshire, wealthy merchants in York, Beverley and other towns near the sheep pastures of Lincolnshire and the Yorkshire Wolds bought up large supplies of wool and put it out to be carded, spun and woven. Some of it was exported through Hull, and the rest dyed and finished locally. Best blue cloth from Beverley cost £7 a piece (of 24 yards, or about 22 metres) in 1319.

Work was controlled in these and other main districts by craft guilds. Lincoln had a guild of weavers in 1131, and they existed in most other towns by this date or soon after. There were guilds, too, for other trades. An application to the mayor and corporation by the Exeter Guild of Weavers,

Tuckers and Shearmen in 1558 shows why guilds existed. The guild asked for a renewal of their regulations:

> as well for the Commen Weale of the sayd Citie and good Clothe makyng withyn the sayd Citie and countie of Exeter . . . as also for good rule and governaunce to be had and kepte yn the sayd Citie among the same Felowshypp or company of Wevers Tookers and Sheremen.

This guild dated only from 1479, but its activities were the same as those of guilds 300 years older. These were the control of trade within the town for the advantage of all ('the Commen Weale'), the maintenance of good standards of craftsmanship ('good Clothe makyng') and social gatherings of those engaged in the trade of the town.

Guilds were very powerful in medieval towns, and took the place of local government. They jealously guarded the standard of living of their members. Weavers (or other craftsmen) who lived outside the town could not be members of the guild and were not allowed to trade at the town's fairs and markets — there were none outside the towns. Some guilds admitted strangers to trade, but only on payment of a fine.

Standards were maintained in the craft by two means. One was a thorough apprenticeship, normally lasting seven years, and ending in a practical examination in front of guild officials to show that the apprentice understood the working methods and trade secrets of the craft. Only after this could a new member apply to join the guild. The numbers employed in the craft could therefore be tightly controlled, so that production could be limited to keep prices up. Not all apprentices could afford to join the guild when they became eligible because there was a substantial admission fee to be paid. Those that did not join were able to carry on the craft provided they worked for someone else for a wage, but they could not set up on their own or have apprentices. Such men were called journeymen. Each guild had officials called searchers, who could enter the workshop of any member and inspect the standard of work being done. This was a powerful check on poor standards. In several ways, therefore, a guild severely limited the amount of cloth being made (or wool being spun, or whatever the guild covered). They tended to preserve the old ways of doing work, even when new and better ways were found.

There was also a social side to guild activities. Most had a patron saint and a special chapel within the church. The saint's day was a holiday, starting with a service in the church and ending with a feast. Other feasts took place when new members were admitted, after periodic meetings of the members, and as often as possible in between. Apart from these, work was done for a full six days each week for an average of twelve hours a day, and there was no fortnight's holiday in the summer. All guilds combined to present mystery plays at some

15 Some wool merchants became very wealthy, and used their money to build bridges and beautify churches. This graceful church is at Blythburgh in Suffolk, and owes several extensions and its carved, painted and gilded roof to the profitable wool trade.

time in the year, each dramatizing an episode from the Bible that had links with their own work.

In 1164, Henry II collected taxes from the guilds, and the amount they had to pay gives a rough indication of their relative size and influence. The highest sum was £12, paid by the weavers in London. A close second, at £10, were the York weavers. Guilds of weavers in Winchester, Lincoln and Oxford were all assessed at £6, and so too was the fullers' guild in Winchester. £2 was collected from guilds of weavers in Huntingdon and Nottingham. It was natural for the London guild to be larger and wealthier than any others, for it served the country's greatest concentration of population. Wool was constantly passing through the town on its way for export, and could easily be supplied to local weavers. All the other textile towns worth taxing were in major wool producing areas, and were quite large towns by medieval standards.

Two centuries later, there was much more movement of cloth from one district to another. The guilds, though still powerful within the towns, had lost their control over what went on outside them. This was bound to happen at some stage but the actual cause in this case was the need to make more cloth, which could only be done by using fulling stocks. These had to be worked by water power, and there was a limit to the number of mills that could be sited on the short length of river that passed through most towns. Priority went to the corn mills, since each town had to be able to produce all its own flour in case of siege. Competition from corn millers was as nothing, though, compared with the hostility of boatmen having to cope with successive weirs, and the enmity of towns further upstream whose trade was delayed or stopped by weirs built to pond up water for the mills. At first, fulling was incorporated into corn mills — one pair of stocks could quickly handle all that was previously done by foot. This could not last, however, and by the fourteenth century fulling mills were being built in valleys far from the towns that were the traditional centres of the woollen industry. The mills' builders were landowners, who realized that this was one way of making their estates more profitable, as well as providing some work in the area. The lord of the manor of Wakefield built a fulling mill at Sowerby Bridge about 1275, in the hope that work would flow to it — there were few hamlets nearby when it was built. The gamble paid off. This mill, like most of the fulling mills built from this time onwards, was sited on a swift-flowing stream, where there could be no wrangles about rights of way for boats or interference with trade — there was therefore a certain supply of power.

It would have been impossible for weavers in the towns to have taken time off to trail their cloths to such remote mills for fulling. Instead, the guilds lost control of cloth manufacturing outside their towns, and the industry developed rapidly around the fulling mills.

Regional Differences

The organization of the cloth industry varied greatly from region to region. In the West Country, for example, production came under the control of a small number of wealthy merchant-manufacturers. These men were able to buy up substantial quantities of wool at the annual sales after shearing in the summer, and to store it in warehouses. Although they understood the processes involved in making cloth, they did none of it themselves but instead put the wool out in small quantities each week to be spun by women in the cottages. The work was frequently scattered among many villages in the locality. After spinning, the

yarn was collected up and distributed to the smaller number of weavers, who also lived in villages and fitted the weaving around their farming tasks. Spinners and weavers were paid a wage for their work. The cloth was then collected and handed to the dyers and bleachers if it was to be finished in Britain, and all of it was taken to the miller for fulling. The men in these crafts were full-time workers who had served apprenticeships, and had workshops near the merchant's home, so that he could supervise the work closely. Some merchants were members of the Company of Merchant Venturers, and could sell the cloth abroad themselves. Others were not, and either sold to those who were or in markets for use in Britain. More woollen cloth was used in Britain than was exported, and many manufacturers were content to supply the home market.

In West Yorkshire journeymen left the towns and built homes near the mills. This led to the rapid growth of villages into towns, such as Bradford, Barnsley and Pontefract, while by 1474 Halifax had become the principal cloth market in West Yorkshire. The merchants in these towns were only interested in buying cloth, arranging for it to be dyed according to the needs of customers, and selling it either in England or exporting it through Hull, Bristol and the Blackwell Hall and Leadenhall markets in London. A narrow cloth used about a quarter of the wool that went into a broadcloth, and the wool available in Yorkshire was poor and cheap. The weavers could therefore afford to buy enough wool to make a piece, with the children carding, the women spinning and the father weaving on a handloom in the bedroom, where most light could fall on the loom. The clothier, as he called himself, took the cloth down to the mill for fulling, then home to stretch back to shape on a tenter frame, and finally to a cloth market in one of the towns. One of the authorized markets was Almondbury, where cloth was sold on the flat-topped tombs in the churchyard. The clothiers in Yorkshire were independent of merchants — they decided when they would weave and when farm, and how much they would weave and to what design. They still had to work ten, twelve and fourteen hours a day for a meagre profit but at least they had the satisfaction of seeming to be their own masters. Some clothiers owned their homes, looms and everything, others rented home or loom, and some weavers were content to be journeymen in other people's houses. It made a complex pattern that was always changing, as the demand for different kinds of cloth varied.

Regional differences in how the work was managed were matched by varieties of cloth. Though the West Country was famed for its export quality broadcloths, some narrow cloths called kerseys were also made, and flannel too. Welsh flannel was more famous, especially red, and was woven in farmhouses throughout the principality. A small suplus was carried into Chester

16 (*Opposite*) Cropping woollen cloth, sixteenth century. Fulled cloth was very shaggy when it dried, and would not have made attractive clothes. The surplus fibre was raised by brushing the cloth with teazles on the frame against the wall, and then cropped with heavy iron shears. This was a skilled and dusty job.

or down the River Severn to Bristol for export. Kerseys, penistones, everlastings, northern dozens and other types of narrow cloth were made in Yorkshire, and cheap quality friezes and 'cottons' (made of wool even so) were all that the wool in Lancashire would produce. Kendal cloth was little better, and sold for 4½d (2p) a yard in the fifteenth century. Tartans were the main product of Scotland, though few of these had achieved the rich variety of colour and pattern that they were to have later.

The odd district out in this was East Anglia, where the worsted yarn was spun. This required different preparation, and originally had been made under the guidance of Dutch immigrants. Instead of carding, the wool was passed through long-toothed combs that needed to be heated over charcoal fires (warm fibres slide more easily). The short fibres were combed out (and used to make woollen yarn) and after the combing the long ones lay straight and parallel. When spun, they made a fine yarn which wove into a cloth that was thinner than woollen cloth, but just as strong and warm without any need of fulling. Woollen cloth had a felted appearance, but on worsted stuff every yarn could be seen, allowing the design of a new range of patterns. The skill of worsted-making lay in combing, and the guilds of combers in Norwich and other towns ruled the trade.

The best wool for combing came from Lincolnshire sheep, and the industry grew up in the East Anglian counties of Norfolk, Suffolk and Essex. The cloth is traditionally associated with the village of Worstead in Norfolk, and with the skill of Dutch immigrants. In the twelfth and thirteenth centuries, several kinds of worsted were being woven. The two most popular, though expensive, were says which were made of fine yarns and were very delicate, and serges, a rather thicker cloth used for curtains, wall hangings and outer clothes.

Worsted-making spread to Yorkshire and Lancashire later, and perhaps to other areas also. The industry ran into difficulties at the beginning of the sixteenth century because of the design of new fabrics in Holland. These new draperies, as they were called, were similar to worsted cloth but more popular, so that an annual export of between 5,000 and 8,000 pieces of worsted in the 1520s fell to a mere 1,000 in the 1540s. Yorkshire worsted-makers turned to wool instead, while East Anglia had severe unemployment for many years. Elizabeth I encouraged Dutch workers to bring the secrets of the new draperies with them to England, and East Anglia was transformed once again into a prosperous area. The growth in the production of new draperies came after 1600, however, and belongs more to the next chapter.

Royal Help

Elizabeth's encouragement to immigrants is an example of deliberate government aid to the textile industry as a whole which was offered from time to time. Such aid seldom took the form of putting money directly into the industry. A rare exception was Henry III, who bought 1,000 ells (1,250 yards or 1,143 metres) of fine linen in both Sussex and Wiltshire in 1253 to encourage the industry. The more usual kinds of royal help were the incentives given to immigrants with new skills, laws to force increased or different production methods, and help with overseas trade. Henry IV, for example, dispatched two ambassadors to boost the sale of English cloth abroad:

> After the arrival of the English ambassadors in the land of Prussia, it was ordained that from the eighth day of October in the year of Our Lord 1405, all English merchants whatsoever should have free liberty to arrive with all kinds of their merchandise in whatsoever part of the land of Prussia, and to make sale of them, as hath heretofore from ancient times been accustomed.

The agreement came to a sudden end the next year, but it did show that the king knew what would benefit him and manufacturers best. Later kings made trade treaties with whatever countries they could, to boost the sale of cloths.

Many treaties offered no more than an opening to merchants, assuring them of a safe passage. A variety of trading companies were set up in the sixteenth century to exploit such treaties, and were frequently successful. In the 1550s, the Company of the Merchants Adventurers to Russia sent out three ships full of goods, with detailed instructions to their agents:

> You shall receive, God willing, out of the said good ships, these kinds of wares following, all marked with the general mark of the Company as followeth: 25 fardels containing 207 sorting cloths, one fine violet in grain, and one scarlet, and 40 cottons for wrappers, . . . 500 pieces of Hampshire kerseys, 9 barrels of pewter. You are to receive our said goods, and to procure the sales to our most advantage either for ready money, time or barter: having consideration that you do make good debts, and also foreseeing that you barter to profit, and for such wares as be here most vendible, as wax, tallow, train oil, hemp and flax. Of furs we desire no great plenty, because they be dead wares.

In 1561, kerseys were being sold in Persia for the Society of the Merchant Adventurers for the Discovery of Lands and Islands, and a growing number of companies were active in most parts of the world. Edward III had started an interest in the export of textiles, which was pursued with accelerating interest throughout the period of this chapter.

A report from one of the agents of such a company in the 1580s spoke of 'a certain little tree' in Persia which grew cotton 'like a fleece of wool'. Neither flock masters, clothiers nor merchants lost a night's sleep over the report, but they were soon to lose much more than that.

5. All Change

The period of this chapter, 1600-1750, was a time of upheaval. The glorious days of 'Good Queen Bess' gave way to a growing mistrust between king and parliament as the House of Commons began to assert its importance. The result was the Civil War which broke out in 1642, led to the execution of Charles I in 1649, and smouldered on through the protectorate of Oliver Cromwell. The Civil War was a social disaster, as friends and families fought on opposing sides. It damaged trade and industry while it lasted, and although it encouraged those

17 Clothiers took their cloth to market on the backs of pack animals, and brought back the raw wool for the next piece. The horses seem unhappy, and some of the weavers had to help carry the cloth themselves.

industries that were necessary for fighting, it discouraged many others. It did speed up the spread of new ideas, though, as armies travelled from one region to another.

The royal family was brought back to England under Charles II in 1660, though parliament retained the power to govern the country. Political upheavals followed, with the exile of James II after a revolution in 1688, and a long succession of wars with France and other countries from 1689 to 1815.

In such a time of political and social upheaval, it was inevitable that there would be great changes in textile fashions and taste. However, many of the swings in fortune affecting particular fabrics were caused by quite different factors. One of these was a steady growth in the wealth of the country, and the development of many other industries to join wool as major exporters. Another was the 'certain little tree' that grew cotton. Changes in fashion also played a part.

New Draperies

There were estimated to be 3,000 Dutch and Walloons in Norwich in 1569, and others settled in Lancashire and other traditional textile areas. They brought with them the latest fashions, and the knowledge of how to make them. Most important among these were the new draperies, a most descriptive name: they were a new mixture of yarns, and they made up into better-looking clothes because they were thinner and so folded (draped) better than the thick woollen cloths. The better drape came from the use of fine yarns — all worsted cloths draped well. What was new was that worsted yarns were only used for the warp, while fine woollen yarn formed the weft. The result was that far more exciting patterns were woven than had been usual before, and clothes became brighter. They were lighter in weight too, because of the finer yarns being used.

Every pattern had its own name, and the list of the new draperies could continue for several pages. Some of the more common were bays, russells, perpetuanas, shalloons and tammies; there were also frisadoes, minikins, bombasines, grograines, buffins, mockadoes and many more besides. All the cloths were lighter in weight than woollen cloths, and some of them were as thin as linen. Many of them were exported to Mediterranean countries — shalloons, for example, were frequently dyed scarlet and sent to Turkey. 'Bombazine' was a word used in France for the cotton cloth made in the east: much of the woollen bombasine made in Britain in the seventeenth century was woven in Lancashire.

England was in a good position to make these cloths because it had more plentiful supplies of suitable wool than most countries. These supplies increased during the course of the seventeenth century because of a slow but progressive change in the wool grown by English sheep. From being short, curly and ideally suited to making woollen cloth, it became long and straighter.

41

Woollen manufacturers were indignant but helpless, while anyone making worsted yarn was delighted. Exports of wool were banned to deny competitors in other countries the advantage of it.

Production of new draperies therefore increased steadily throughout the century. At first the industry developed most quickly in East Anglia, where many of the immigrants had settled and where there was a tradition of making worsted cloth. New draperies were popular, though, and weavers in many areas soon began to make them — not all the immigrants stayed in East Anglia. The new cloths were being made in the West Country by 1604, and Coventry had become the centre of tammy-making by mid-century. Tammies were lighter than some of the other fabrics, and were used for ladies' clothing.

In the 1680s, weavers in Lancashire and West Yorkshire began to make some of the cheaper kinds of new drapery, at the expense of manufacturers in the West Country and East Anglia. Lancashire was well placed to take advantage of a growing trans-Atlantic trade. Imports of Indian cotton cloth dwindled at this time, and Lancashire weavers made a successful alternative called callimancos. These were woven with brightly coloured stripes and checks, and some even had silk flowers woven in, while others were printed. These weavers complained loudly when cotton cloth was again imported after 1700, but soon realized that it would be better to make what the public wanted than complain because it did not want what they made.

By 1700, the term 'new draperies' was being abandoned, and the wide range of cloths were simply described as worsteds. These formed the bulk of the textiles exported at this time, though far more woollen cloth was actually being made. Production of worsteds continued to grow in East Anglia, but grew much faster in West Yorkshire. Halifax had become the centre of worsted weaving by 1750, Wakefield had replaced Coventry as the home of tammies, and towns like Bradford, Leeds, Bingley and Keighley were rapidly giving up woollen cloth production in favour of worsteds. It was about this time that Yorkshire drew level with East Anglia in the value of output; by 1770, East Anglia produced worsteds valued at £1.2 million, but Yorkshire's output was reckoned to be £1.4 million. Fifty years later, Yorkshire was almost the only worsted manufacturing area, and East Anglia was unable to compete.

Wool

The woollen manufacturers no longer had everything their own way, as had been the case since the fourteenth century. The popularity of worsteds and imported cotton inevitably affected sales of woollen cloth, and the steady deterioration in the quality of English wool undermined the quality of the finished cloth. This was particularly serious for the West Country manufacturers, whose broadcloths had been made of the best wool. A fall in quality immediately affected the export trade.

18 This portrait of Charles I shows him wearing some of the more expensive fabrics. His ruff is made from several layers of lace. The cloth is a worsted, with silk woven in to create the design. The sleeves are lined with silk to show through the slits.

It was therefore very strange that one man was allowed to disrupt the export trade completely. Sir William Cockayne, who had invented a new way of dyeing and finishing cloth, persuaded James I (1603-25) to ban the export of undyed cloth and so force English dyers to improve the quality of their work. The Merchant Adventurers were stopped from exporting white cloths in 1614, and Cockayne formed a company to buy all the white cloth intended for export, to dye and finish it, and then to export it. It was hoped that this would boost the income from customs duties in much the same way as Edward III's ban on the export of raw wool had done over three centuries before.

Instead, the entire woollen industry was disrupted because the new company could not find any buyers for their finished goods in Europe. The quality was not up to that of the Flemish dyers, who bought cloth wherever they could and sold all they dyed. Exports from London for January-March 1615 were 46 per cent down on the same months of 1614. The company stopped buying cloth, weavers were left starving and all was chaos. A letter written within four months of the start of Cockayne's scheme describes the situation:

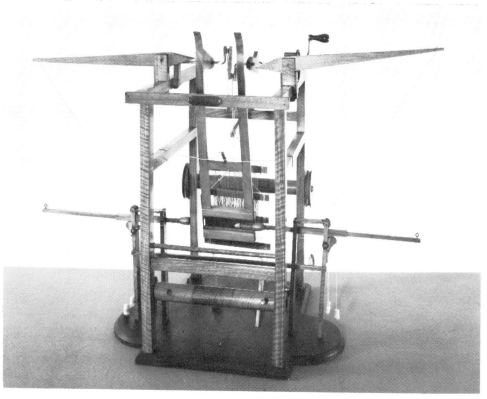

19 A model of a power loom invented by a French naval officer called de Gennes in 1677. It was designed to be installed in windmills, so the drive-shaft (indicated by a handle) is at the top. The shuttle was passed from side to side on the long arms, each with a spring-loaded cup to hold it. The idea is very similar to mid-twentieth century rapier looms, but was not put into use at the time.

The great project of dieing and dressinge of cloth is at a stand, and they knowe not well how to go forward nor backward, for the clothiers do generally complain that theyre clothe lies on theyre hands, and the clotheworkers and diers wearie the Kinge and counsaile with petitions, wherein they complaine that they are in worse case than before, . . . and indeed yt is found that there hath not been a cloth died or dressed since Christmass more than usual . . . whereby the Customes do fall, and many other inconveniences follow both at home and abroade, whiles the new companions [Cockayne's company] differ amongst themselves and draw dyvers wages, so that the old companie [Merchant Adventurers] hath been dealt withall to resume the trade, and set al straight again, yf yt may be.

But it could not. The scheme was abandoned in 1617, and the Merchant Adventurers were given wider powers than ever before in the hope that they could win back lost customers. They, however, were satisfied with the cloth they could buy from Flanders and neighbouring countries, and were no longer interested in white English cloth. A severe depression in the woollen industry followed in the 1620s, when much less cloth was sold than usual, and many spinners and weavers were out of work.

Clothiers making cloth for use in Britain had recovered from the depression by the end of the 1620s. Woollen cloth was the cheapest fabric available, and the only kind that most people could afford. It was still produced in most counties, and many families continued to make their own. This system was beginning to break down, however, as more and more people combined farming with some other industrial work, and bought their cloth in the market. Either way, a major part of the woollen cloth made was used within Britain, and this part of the industry could never be depressed for long.

The pinch was felt by those who relied on exporting their cloth. The West Country merchant-manufacturers were the hardest hit, for they had most to lose. They tried to secure privileges that would encourage trade in their kinds of cloth but these did not greatly help. There was little that could be done to boost a trade that was going out of fashion except turn to making the more fashionable worsteds. Local wools were unsuitable for this which, with its total lack of experience in the craft, put the region at a disadvantage.

The other principal exporting region, West Yorkshire, was in a better position to ride out the storm of change. The growth of worsted-making in the area meant that people could change from one textile to the other as trade varied. Changes in trade were not as complete as with broadcloths, because most of the Yorkshire cloths were cheap, hardwearing kersies which were sold in all parts of Europe. This again was the cloth used by most of the population, especially in mid-European countries, and the demand for it did not fluctuate as much as the trade in more expensive cloths. Another advantage of making woollens and worsteds in the same area was that the short fibres (called noils), combed out from the long fibres (tops) used for worsted spinning, were the kind preferred for woollens. Daniel Defoe visited the area around Halifax in 1725:

After we had mounted the third hill, we found the country . . . one continued village . . . hardly a house standing out of a speaking distance from another, and . . . we could see that almost at every house there was a tenter, and almost on every tenter a piece of cloth, or kersey, or shalloon, for they are the three articles of that country's labour; . . . look which way we would, high to the tops and low to the bottoms, it was all the same; innumerable houses and tenters, and a white piece upon every tenter.

(The 'cloth' was broadcloth, though not of the same quality as that made in the

20 A weaver's cottage, built in 1671. The long row of windows on the ground floor provide light for the looms. The upstairs windows were enlarged at a later date, when it became more normal to weave on the upper floor instead.

West Country.) By weaving worsted shalloons and also broad and narrow woollen cloths, Yorkshire manufacturers could always be sure of being able to sell something.

By the end of the seventeenth century, the woollen industry was back in full production. Spanish wool had to be imported for the weft of the better quality cloths, and growing quantities of Irish wool too. Woollen manufacturers could no longer rely on the English woolsack, which was steadily becoming the property of the worsted makers. Woollen merchants had also learned that, now that they were no longer the only cloth-makers in the country, they could not expect to have everything their own way in future. Yet despite all the upsets, the manufacture of woollen cloth continued to employ most people, use most wool and supply more cloth for export than any other branch of textiles. An industry as vast as the woollen industry had been in the sixteenth century could contract a very long way and still remain larger than any other.

A new branch of the industry became more important after 1650 — the making of blankets. Traditionally people had made their blankets for themselves (if they had them at all), but specialist blanket makers, concentrated in a few areas in the seventeenth century, became increasingly important.

A description of the industry in one area will illustrate how it operated in others. Doctor Robert Plot wrote about the blankets made in the Oxfordshire town of Witney in 1677, which were

> esteemed so far beyond all others, that this place has engrossed the whole trade of the Nation for this Commodity; in so much that the wool fit for their use, which is chiefly fell wool (off from Sheepskins) centers here from some of the furthermost parts of the Kingdom, *viz,* from Rumney-marsh, Canterbury, Colchester, Norwich, Exeter, Leicester, Northampton, Coventry, Huntingdon, etc, of which the Blanketers, whereof there are Threescore [60] in this town, that amongst them have at least 150 looms, employing 3,000 poor people, from children of eight years old to decrepit old age, do work out above a hundred packs of wool per week. This Fell wool they separate into five or six sorts . . . Long fell wool they send to Wells, Taunton, Tiverton, *etc*, for making worsted stockings; of head wool and bay wool they make the Blankets of 12, 11 and 10 quarters broad [1 quarter = 9 inches, or 22.9 cm] and sometimes send it, if it bear a good price, to Kidderminster for making their stuffs, and to Evesham, Parshore, etc, for making yarn stockings; or into Essex for making Bays . . . of the ordinary and middle they make blankets of 8 and 7 quarters broad; and of these mixt with the coarser locks of fleece wool, a sort of stuff they call Duffields [duffel] . . . of which Duffields and blankets consists the chief trade of Witney.

The blanket trade, as with all the woollen industry, continued to function and even expand up to 1750. Some manufacturers were alarmed at the popularity of calico, but few saw any threat in that.

Linen and Cotton
The linen industry continued at much the same size throughout this period as it had been for some centuries, increasing production in step with the slow growth in the population. Linen was made wherever flax grew in quantity, such as in the villages near Glasgow, Manchester, Knaresborough, Carlisle, Leicester, Derby, Reading, and in several parts of Somerset and Devon. The crop was only a few thousand tons a year, so yarn was imported from Ireland and Scotland, and some flax from Russia.

Linen was expensive in the seventeenth century, and there were far fewer customers for it than for wool. Production was best organized around Manchester, where linen drapers bought the raw materials and put them out to weavers, who in turn employed local women and children for carding and spinning. The cloth was dyed and finished by specialist finishers, who had workshops in Manchester and Salford.

Processing cotton developed in the more active linen manufacturing areas,

21 Eighteenth-century bleachfields. Before the 1790s, there was still no other way to bleach fabric than to boil it up, adding sour milk or some other acid, and then to lay it out to dry in the sun. Larger bleachfields were set out in the eighteenth century, with boiling sheds to one side.

where people were used to handling fine yarns. Raw cotton may have been imported and manufactured in the sixteenth century, and certainly was by 1610. By 1640, cotton from Cyprus and Smyrna was being brought into the London docks, sent to Lancashire and Cheshire to be made up like linen, and then returned to London. Much of it was used to make a cloth called a fustian, which had a linen warp but a cotton weft. Hardly any cotton cloth was made, and the little that was was of poor quality.

Cotton cloth was becoming increasingly popular, though, due mainly to the East India Company. This trading company brought into Britain an Indian cloth called calico. This was all cotton, and was printed in bright colours and attractive patterns. It was expensive because of the distance it was carried but there was nothing available that could compare with it — wool could not be printed. Its popularity caused concern to the manufacturers of thin woollen cloths, such as those used for flannel petticoats, which people were ignoring in preference for cotton. The size and wealth of the woollen industry gave it some influence in parliament, and it used this to obtain protective laws. An act in 1700 banned imports of printed fabrics. The result of this was to encourage

22 An engraving of the Lombes' celebrated silk mill on the River Derwent near Derby. The water wheels have been supplemented by steam power. The mill was copied by other silk manufacturers, but did not lead to developments in the manufacture of any other textiles at that time.

merchants to buy plain cotton cloth and dyers to learn how to print it. Customers did not want the imitation cottons made of worsted, referred to earlier; they wanted the real thing. A more complete act followed in 1721, which prohibited the buying, selling, wearing or owning of cotton cloth. It did not, however, stop merchants from importing raw cotton, and the English manufacturers were encouraged to improve on the clumsy efforts they had made before.

It needed the combined output of five or six spinners to keep one weaver at work. Any increase in output was severely restricted by the shortage of spinners, and this was made worse when John Kay devised an attachment for a handloom to allow one man to weave broadcloth by himself. Though invented in 1733, the flying shuttle was not used much until the shortage of yarn was overcome by machinery. John Wyatt and Lewis Paul patented a cotton spinning machine in 1738, and opened a factory in Birmingham with one of these machines. The venture was not a success, and the inventiveness of others was needed to make the machine effective.

The cotton industry grew from small beginnings to become, by 1750, an

49

23 A knitting frame of the kind used widely in the east Midlands. Knitting was done by a combined series of hand and foot movements, working from patterns known by heart or noted in highly prized books. A dozen such frames are still in use today to make the more complex patterns that no modern machine can copy.

established though barely legal occupation. Another act was passed in 1735 which exempted fustian from the ban of 1721, and it was not long before that act was ignored, even though it was not repealed until 1774. Cotton producing, though, still formed only a very small fraction of the textile trade. Its consumption of raw cotton doubled between 1700 and 1750, but cotton manufacturing remained a dwarf to the giant woollen industry and substantial worsted trade. Given machinery, however, a breakthrough was possible.

Silk
Silk worms have never flourished in the English climate, and until the seventeenth century silk cloth had to be imported, making it an expensive luxury fabric. In 1685, a large number of Protestants had to flee for their lives from Catholic France, when the protection they had been given by the Edict of Nantes was suddenly removed. Many of these arrived in England, and among them were some skilled silk weavers who set up small workshops in London.

50

The families lived near each other in Spitalfields, which became the centre of British silk weaving. It was a good base for the industry, since all the silk was imported from Italy and came through the port of London.

At that time Italian silk was cheap, but it became more expensive as the volume of silk woven in Britain grew. It was imported as 'thrown' silk: the filaments of silk unwound from the cocoon were too fine to use singly, so several were twisted around each other to make a thicker thread, a process called throwing. (Much later, short lengths and other waste was spun to make a cheaper thread, but thrown silk was always of better quality.) The rising price of Italian thrown silk encouraged John Lombe to find alternatives. Nothing was known about the machinery the Italians used, so Lombe set off in 1716, managed to find his way into an Italian throwing workshop and made furtive drawings. These he smuggled out of Italy in rolls of silk, and only narrowly escaped himself after a sea chase.

Safely back in Britain after this first recorded piece of industrial espionage, Lombe rented the town hall and some other buildings in Derby and proceeded to set up machines based on his drawings. His thrown silk was very much cheaper than that of the Italians, and he was soon able to build a factory so large that it was still being talked of as a marvel 50 years later. It was built near Derby on an island in the River Derwent, and was 5 storeys high, 150 metres long and had 460 windows — the kind of size normally reserved for cathedrals. It was packed with machinery, powered by a large water wheel. The machines were built for adults to work, but many children were employed as well. Some of them had problems reaching the machines, like William Hutton, who started work at the mill in 1730, aged seven:

> It was found upon trial that nature had not given me length sufficient to reach the engine [machine]; for, out of three hundred persons employed at the mill, I was by far the least and the youngest . . . A pair of high pattens were therefore fabricated, and tied fast about my feet, to make them steady companions. They were clumsy companions, which I dragged about one year, and with pleasure delivered up.

John Lombe died soon after he had built the mill (it was rumoured that he had been poisoned by an Italian woman sent over to exact revenge), and his brother took over. When the Lombes' patents ran out, other throwing mills were set up in Stockport, Macclesfield and Sheffield, and weaving developed in these towns as well as being firmly established in London.

Knitting

The use of machines that could duplicate people's skills was paralleled in knitting. This was in many ways more important than silk production, for men and women alike had worn stockings since the Middle Ages. The only way that these could be made was by knitting them, because they had to fit the shape of a leg, and the fabric had to have some stretch in it to make it fit well. All stockings had to be knitted by hand. Most families made their own (just as many now make their own sweaters and cardigans) but some people made more than they needed and sold the surplus.

By the end of the sixteenth century, there was a growing shortage in the supply of knitted stockings for sale and this prompted a clergyman, William Lee, to find a way round the problem. By 1589, he had perfected a knitting frame which could do all that a hand knitter could do but faster. It was worked by hand, and the frame knitter had to become very skilled if he was to master the more intricate patterns. William Lee was in immediate trouble. Hand knitters were afraid they would lose the money they had made from their knitting, and hounded Lee until he fled to France. Those who worked with him there returned to Britain after his death, and began to work the machines in Nottingham.

There was no trouble this time, and many frames were soon in use, knitting stockings and shawls from woollen and worsted yarns, with silk and cotton added later. Frames were small, much smaller than a loom, and so they could be used in people's homes. Unlike looms, though, the frames were expensive, far more than a knitter could afford. A system soon developed by which the merchants supplied both the frame and the yarn; the knitter was paid a wage for his work less rent for the use of the frame. This was fast becoming a scandalous system by the beginning of the eighteenth century, with merchants only paying wages for work done but collecting a full rent each week whether they had given work or not.

The knitting frame was one of the first machines to replace the skill of people's hands. Lombe's mill was the first building to assemble a large number of workers under one roof, with some specializing in one job and others in another. Neither of these developments got very far in their own industries, but both were blended to produce the revolution that transformed the cotton industry after 1750.

6. King Cotton

The period of this chapter, 1750-1914, was, for textiles, the age of cotton. The industry exploded in the second half of the eighteenth century, and continued to expand throughout the nineteenth. Manufacturers changed from making coarse cotton goods, inferior to what was being made elsewhere, into supplying quality cottons to the entire world. The growth of the industry was an undoubted success story for technology, whose advances were of more immediate help to cotton than to other fibres. The new methods were in time adapted to most other fibres, but the layout of this chapter underlines the leading role played by the cotton masters among the textile manufacturers.

24 When cotton was king. Apart from its cheapness, one of the main attractions of cotton cloth was the cheerful patterns that could be printed on it in bright colours. At first this was done with hand blocks, but copper printing cylinders came into use after about 1840.

25 Spinning on the great wheel, nineteenth century. Grandmother in the corner is reeling off the spun yarn into hanks.

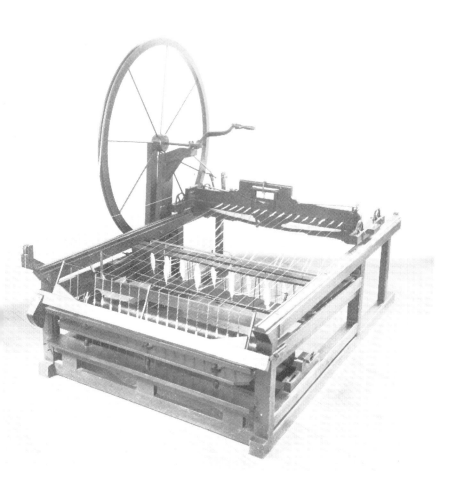

26 James Hargreaves's spinning jenny was at first made small enough to be used in a cottage, in place of the great wheel. Later versions were larger and installed in mills, but were often still hand powered.

Machines

The output of cotton yarn could not increase in the eighteenth century until ways were found to replace skills that took years to learn with machines that could be operated after a short training. The organization required to supply women spinning in their cottages with raw materials and collect up the yarn had reached its limits in any case, at a time when transport was appallingly slow. There was a permanent shortage of spinners, which had prevented any widespread use of the flying shuttle.

The first successful spinning machine was invented by James Hargreaves in 1765. Cotton, like the wool used in woollens, was short fibred, and it had normally been spun on the great wheel. Hargreaves adapted the wheel so that it could make more than one thread at a time, by adding more spindles. The machine was called the spinning jenny (spinning engine was the correct phrase). It was still worked by hand — most jennies were made small enough to be driven by children, since the skill required to draw out the fibres was built into the machine. This development brought new prosperity to spinners working at home, and helped to relieve at least part of the yarn shortage. Like all yarn spun on the great wheel, yarn spun on the jenny was loose and soft, which made it suitable for the weft but too breakable for warp threads.

Richard Arkwright overcame this problem in 1768 with a machine which he claimed was his own invention. This had been developed from the machine made by Wyatt and Paul in the 1730s, and was based on the principle of the Saxony wheel. Arkwright's machine was called the water frame, for only water power could make it work. The yarn it produced was fine and strong, just what was needed for warps. This machine compelled cotton merchants to build special mills, since it could not be used in a cottage. Arkwright started with some water frames in Nottingham but soon built a much larger mill on the River Derwent at Cromford. This was the first of the many mills that were going to boost the output of the industry. Arkwright later invented a machine to card the cotton rather than having it done by hand, and arranged the machinery so that the cotton passed from one machine to the next with the minimum of handling. He was taken to court over his claim to have invented the water frame, and was deprived of the patent in 1785. But he was already well established and the loss did not worry him, any more than it proved the identity of the real inventor.

The last spinning machine to be designed at this time was made by Samuel Crompton in 1779. He took the working methods of the two other machines and combined them, the result being called the mule. The yarn it spun was equally suitable for warp or weft, and the machine could be made small enough to be worked by hand in a cottage, or large enough to justify building a factory and installing power. Crompton could not afford to patent his machine and made it public in 1780. Many manufacturers promised to subscribe towards

27 Carded wool and cotton made better yarns, and in the nineteenth century the carding engine replaced hand cards (*see* illustration **10**). Fibres fed in from the right were worked by rollers covered in fine wire teeth, revolving against a similarly covered drum. The carded fibres were combed off into slivers at the left.

paying for it, but business ethics have frequently been a blot on industrial societies, and he was in fact paid very little. The mule was soon widely used, mostly in factories. Within 20 years, mules of more than 400 spindles were being built, making possible an unheard of increase in output. By this time American cotton was also cheaper and more plentiful.

The increase in spun cotton was so great that by the 1780s weaving had become the bottleneck. Handloom weavers abandoned weaving woollens and worsteds to turn to the more profitable cottons, and could expect wages of a guinea (£1.05) a piece. Weavers in Bury strutted around with £5-notes stuck in their hatbands. They would have been less confident had they known that Edmund Cartwright, a clergyman who had never seen a loom, was in fact busy inventing a power loom. He patented it in 1785, and installed several in an animal powered mill in Doncaster two years later. The machine did not work well, and many were broken up by angry weavers afraid of losing their incomes.

The loom was improved and began to be used for coarse cottons from 1793, but its widespread use came later. This, with the spinning machines and others for scribbling, willeying, piecening and several other processes, made possible a rapid increase in cotton production, provided the right methods could be found.

Richard Arkwright was a pioneer in this respect too. The water frame already made it inevitable that future developments would be in mills, which offered many advantages over domestic working. The time wasted carrying small quantities from place to place was reduced at once, and better use was made of people's time. Supervision of work was possible in a factory, which led to better or certainly more even quality. It also meant that patterns could be kept secret. Other advantages came with machines, whose output was far greater than was possible in a cottage, especially when they were driven by water power, and later by steam. Arkwright realized that his workers would become more skilful in their work if they specialized on one machine or at one process, instead of turning their hand to everything, as was the case among people working at home. He also insisted on keeping careful records of goods bought and sold, wages paid and similar matters, in order to have a clear overall picture of what was going on in so large an enterprise. His ideas on specialization of labour and proper book-keeping became normal practice in later mills.

New Mills
The raw cotton imported for use in Britain amounted to 1,000 tonnes in 1750. This figure rose slowly to 3,000 tonnes by 1780, and then the boom began. The total manufactured in 1790 was 13,800 tonnes, which rose to 23,000 tonnes in 1800, and passed 45,000 tonnes (100 million lbs) for the first time in

28 Samuel Crompton built the mule at his home in Bolton, and tried to keep it a secret, but the finer quality of the yarns he took to market made other spinners curious. At first the mule was a cottage machine (as here) but it was soon made larger (*see illustration* **30**).

Protection

FOR THE

INDUSTRIOUS

Weavers.

INFORMATION having been received that a great number of industrious Weavers have been deterred by threats and acts of violence from the pursuit of their lawful occupations, and that in many instances their Shuttles have been taken, and their Materials damaged by persons acting under the existing Combinations :

Notice is hereby Given,

That every Protection will be afforded to persons so injured, upon giving Information to the Constables of Stockport : And a Reward of

FIFTY GUINEAS

Will be paid, on conviction, to the person who will come forward with such evidence as may be the means of convicting any one or more of the offences mentioned in the Act of Parliament, of which an Extract is subjoined : And a Reward of

TWENTY GUINEAS

Will be paid, on conviction, to the person who will come forward and inform of any person being guilty of assaulting or molesting industrious and honest Weavers, so as to prevent them from taking out or bringing in their Work peaceably.

PETER BROWN, }
T. CARTWRIGHT, } *CONSTABLES.*

Stockport, June 17th, 1808.

By the 22nd, Geo. 3, C. 40, S. 3.

It is enacted, " That if any person enter, by force, into any House or Shop, with intent to Cut and Destroy any Linen or Cotton, or Linen and Cotton mixed with any other Materials, in the Loom, or any Warp or Shute, Tools, Tackle, and Utensils, or shall Cut or Destroy the same, or shall Break and Destroy any Tools, Tackle, or Utensils, for Weaving, Preparing, or Making any such Manufactures, every such Offender shall be guilty of FELONY, without Benefit of Clergy".

J. CLARKE, PRINTER.

29 The handloom weavers of cotton cloth were the first to feel the effects of mechanization. Many were put out of work when power looms were installed in mills, and they were bitter enough about the looms and those who worked them to raid mills, break machines, spoil cloth and threaten workers. Employers were keen to discourage this.

1810. Increases of this magnitude could only have been handled by mill methods.

Mills were built first in Nottinghamshire and Derbyshire, and near the main importing centres of London, Bristol, Liverpool and Glasgow. By the 1790s these last two were becoming the dominant areas of cotton cloth production, while the Midlands counties produced yarn for the stocking knitters and the new lace mills. Glasgow and Liverpool had clear advantages as cotton centres — they were the main ports for trade with America (the source of most raw cotton by 1790), there was plentiful soft water for washing the cloth, they were both areas where linen production had trained people in weaving fine fabrics, and coal was readily available for heating dyeing vats and for steam power. Lancashire and north Cheshire emerged as the main cotton cloth district. Of 35 steam engines bought by cotton manufacturers in the years 1790-1800, 29 were installed in Lancashire, and 20 mills were built in and near Manchester alone in 1802. A visitor to Lancashire in 1810 could have been forgiven for thinking he had seen the cotton industry, for he had certainly seen most of it.

30 (*Above*) The superior quality of yarn spun on mules encouraged machine makers to build them larger. They were set up in mills in pairs, close together. Note the awkward working conditions — the continual movement as the carriage went back and forth, the open gas flames on the walls and the lack of safety guards.

31 (*Below*) Except for the scattered silk mills, few people knew what a factory was until the rash of cotton mills began appearing in the 1770s. This one in Cheshire is typical of most, as is the state of transport, which did not match the scale of the mills until railways were built.

The rapid transformation that had come over the industry was not lost on people living at the time. Edward Baines wrote in 1835:

A cotton-spinning establishment offers a remarkable example of how, by the use of very great power, an enormous quantity of the easiest work can be accomplished. Often we may see in a single building a 100 horse-power steam engine which has the strength of 880 men, set in motion 50,000 spindles besides all the auxiliary machines. The whole requires the service of but 750 workers. But these machines, with the assistance of that mighty power, can produce as much yarn as formerly could hardly have been spun by 200,000 men, so that one man can now produce as much as formerly required 266! Each spindle produces daily from 2½ to 3 hanks of yarn, and thus the 50,000 together will furnish in 12 hours a thread 62,000 English miles in length — that is to say which could encircle the whole earth 2½ times . . . That one spinner can now produce as much yarn in a single day as formerly in a year, that fabrics can be bleached in two days to a pure white that would formerly have required six or eight months, is the reason why this industry can provide work and bread to incomparably more persons than formerly . . .

The cotton mills certainly did all these things, and paid slightly higher wages than had been the rule when work was done at home. That did not mean, though, that everything was perfect. The cotton towns had sprung up quickly out of villages. There had been no planning, and consequently no provision for water, drainage, decent housing, the making of roads or adequate local government. Conditions at work were poor too — long hours, low pay, awkward positions to work in and danger from machines and tiredness. Life was particularly harsh for the children, employed from the age of seven. None of this was new in itself — children had always worked at home, often starting at an even younger age and with no pay at all. The new feature was that everyone was now herded into a big mill, and it was all remote, strange and disturbing.

The new industrial system had many critics. Luddites attacked the power looms in Lancashire and Cheshire in 1812, and not for the first time. Men like William Cobbett thundered against the slavery of the mills, believing that everyone would be better off if they could go back to being farm labourers. Some of the critics took time to collect facts before they spoke, as will be seen later.

The worst of the conditions were slowly removed. Local government was reformed in 1835, which gave towns powers to correct bad conditions, though it took decades to undo the mistakes of a few years. Factory acts, public opinion and trade unions led to reductions in hours, improved safety standards and compulsory education in the mills. This took time too, and through it all the cotton industry continued to expand. The following table indicates the rate of growth:

average annual imports of raw cotton by decades in thousands of tonnes			
1820s	78	1870s	564
1830s	158	1880s	668
1840s	249	1890s	706
1850s	360	1900s	786
1860s	363	1910s	850

The pattern is one of continuous growth, though the figures hide the cotton famine of 1862-5, when supplies were cut off by the American Civil War. This caused considerable distress, unemployment and bankruptcies, but the industry

32 The architecture of Marshall's flax mill in Leeds was unique — sheep grazed on its flat grass roof. The tall, sombre mills beyond, the tall chimneys, smoke, noise and dirt were the more usual hallmarks of a textile town.

33 A new way of making yarn, ring spinning, was introduced from America in the 1850s. There were no moving carriages, and the frames were economical on both space and effort.

recovered rapidly afterwards. The continuous increase in production was brought about by enlarging mills, installing more powerful engines and employing more workers. An American machine, the ring-spinning frame, began to replace the mule in the 1850s, but there were few other changes. The high tide of the cotton industry was reached in 1912, when 6,700 million square metres of cloth were produced, in addition to yarn. Of that, nearly 6,000 million were exported, to almost every country in the world. Should anything disrupt that export trade, thousands of jobs would immediately be threatened, most of them in Lancashire and Cheshire.

Worsteds
The worsted industry underwent an industrial revolution too, but about 30 years after the cotton manufacturers. There were several reasons for the delay.

34 The first part of the woollen mill in the foreground was started in the eighteenth century. The mill pond provided power for a water wheel. Extensions were designed over the years as new machines became available. The ramshackle appearance is in sharp contrast to the worsted mill in the distance, which was built in the 1840s when all worsted machinery was already available.

One was a shortage of wool combers, which lasted until Edmund Cartwright designed a combing machine in 1792. This was slowly improved over the years, forcing the hand combers to abandon their unhealthy work, and plentiful supplies of combed tops were available by 1830. Another reason was that worsted cloth was much more expensive, and the demand for it rose much more slowly than the demand for cotton.

Slowly, however, it became obvious that more cloth could be sold if it could be made, and the example of the cotton mills seemed to point the way to success. The manufacturers in East Anglia were at an immediate disadvantage. There were none of the swift streams there that the Pennines had, so water power was unobtainable, while any coal for steam power would have to be brought over long distances. West Yorkshire had plentiful water power, and

63

35 Part of the impressive frontage of Titus Salt's mohair mill at Shipley, Yorkshire, built in the 1850s. A canal and railway provided transport at the rear of the mill, and water could be taken from the River Aire nearby.

coal at hand when it was needed. The worsted industry was fairly new in Yorkshire, and was controlled by a small number of merchants who could afford to build mills and buy machinery. They did. Machine spinning began in 1784, using adapted water frames which later came to be called throstles. The period 1780-93 was one of the busiest yet for the Yorkshire worsted makers. Those who made the cheaper cloths were put out of business by the flood of cheap cottons on the market, but exports increased rapidly to compensate, as did the manufacture of luxury goods — yarns for carpets, for example.

The mills confined their work mostly to combing and spinning, while weaving was still done on hand looms. Trade in the cloth halls built from the 1760s onwards had never been better. Wakefield's Tammy Hall was opened in 1766, the Piece Hall at Halifax in 1780, and others in Colne, Penistone and Bradford. Halifax remained the centre of the industry until the 1790s, when Bradford merchants took the lead as a result of their faster change to mill methods.

The career of John Foster in the nineteenth century illustrates the typical change from merchant to manufacturer. He started in a small way, buying yarn from the mills and giving it out from his house to handloom weavers to weave in return for a wage. That was in 1818; soon he had a warehouse in Queensbury from which he continued the same business until 1834. He then decided that it

36 Titus Salt also provided houses for his workers and soon had built up a whole community. Wide streets were lined by varied styles of building, and the church was one of the most ornate ever to be used by Nonconformists.

would pay him to make his own yarn, and used his previous profits to enlarge the warehouse into a mill. By 1836 he was keeping 700 weavers in work, and he continued to enlarge the buildings, in time taking in the weaving side too, until they became the Black Dyke Mills.

Power looms were finally adapted to weave worsted yarns in the 1830s, and were rapidly installed in mills. This finished the last remnants of the East Anglian industry, and entrenched it more firmly in West Yorkshire. Working conditions were similar to those in the cotton mills. Richard Oastler likened the treatment of children in the mills to slavery. Another critic was a Leeds doctor, who treated some of the casualties of mill work. There were frequent outbreaks of fever, and most workers suffered headaches and a loss of appetite from the noise of the machinery, followed by permanent damage to their hearing. Ever present dust and fluff caused lung and breathing diseases. Children were the worst affected for, although they suffered from no definable industrial disease other than looking sickly, Dr Thackrah maintained that the long hours at work exhausted the body's ability to repair itself and robbed children of the possibility of an active old age:

> No man of humanity can reflect without distress on the state of thousands of children, many from six to seven years of age, roused from their beds at an early hour, hurried to the mills, and kept there, with the interval of only 40 minutes, till a late hour at night; kept, moreover, in an atmosphere impure, not only as the air of a town, not only as defective in ventilation, but as loaded also with noxious dust. Health! cleanliness! mental improvement! How are they regarded? Recreation is out of the question. There is scarcely time for meals. The very period of sleep, so necessary for the young, is too often abridged. Nay, children are sometimes worked even in the night. The duration of labour is the opprobrium rather of our manufacturing system than of individuals. The masters with whom I have conversed are men of humanity, and willing, I believe, to adopt any practicable proposal to amend the health and improve the state of their work people. But they are scarcely conscious of the extent of mischief.

That was it: few employers understood what dangers were created by the new processes. And when they did find out, they were often slow to do anything about it, partly because it took time to work out safer ways of doing the same work, and partly because of human nature itself — it takes an exceptional man to make improvements when he is not forced to by outside pressures.

The industry expanded slowly until the 1860s, when a new combing machine invented by two Bradford men in 1851 (G E Donisthorpe and S C Lister) came into general use. This, with the Noble comb invented in 1887, produced more combed tops than were needed for cloth production, and a

65

37 Much woollen cloth was still sold to merchants in cloth halls such as this in the early nineteenth century. Business was conducted in whispers and with the minimum of fuss. Some clothiers designed their own patterns, and sold direct to customers or made to order.

sizeable export trade in yarns was developed. Worsted cloth continued to be popular for men's and ladies' suits, and the industry could rely on a permanent need for the cloth in Britain, most other European countries and America.

Woollens

The woollen manufacturers were surpassed in terms of output by the cotton mills about 1800, and after that were never really in the race. They too adopted new methods, but in an agonizing process spread over a century. As with worsteds, there were reasons for this. One was the technical difficulty of adapting cotton machines to handle the softer woollen fibres. Another was the vast number of separate manufacturers in the industry, and consequently the lack of enough wealthy men to build mills. Yet another, and perhaps the strongest reason, was the hidebound nature of the industry itself, illustrated by this part of a letter written in 1792:

> I want much to prevail upon the manufacturers of wool to be less reserved and mysterious. When they discover any improvement in their art, they keep

38 (*Left*) Until the 1830s, woollen cloth was still cropped by hand. The cloth was raised with teazles (on the far wall), and the shears were weighted to give a closer cut. Cropping workshops were cold, damp and full of dust.

39 (*Opposite*) Timmy was one of the last handloom weavers to make a living from the trade in Yorkshire. He worked at Stanbury, near Haworth. His attic workshop and loom reflect none of the improvements made in the industry in the previous 150 years.

it concealed as much as possible, and, as they all do the same, it has prevented the manufacture of wool from being brought to the same perfection in 500 years that cotton, by a different conduct, has in ten.

There was always a ready sale for woollen cloth in Britain, as well as a reasonable export trade, and this was taken for granted by the manufacturers. Few bothered to think of ways of copying the more progressive textile trades, the 'improvement in their art' was slight, and some could only think of pressing for government protection to shield them from the competition of cheap cottons and worsteds. They were not helped by a swing in fashion away from woollen cloths, which persisted into the 1850s.

As a result, few new mills were built. Instead, as each machine was adapted for wool, like the mule, it was incorporated into the existing fulling mills. Little

TIMMY AT HIS LOOM. F.S.

40 Woollen manufacturers cut costs by recycling fibres recovered from disused clothing and tailors' waste. The bales of shoddy made a comfortable seat while the men posed for the camera.

42 (*Opposite*) The men of St Kilda spent a busy few weeks each summer weaving heavy tweed cloths from wool gathered from the Soay sheep. The cloth paid the rent.

41 (*Below*) When cropping was mechanized, cloth was still raised by teazles, which were now set on large revolving drums. These men are grading and setting teazle heads in iron frames to fit on the drums.

by little, all the processes except those directly to do with weaving became mill work, so that by 1830, the women and children of the family went down to the mill to work, leaving the men at work on the handlooms at home. Power looms were finally adapted for woollens in the 1850s, and new woollen mills began to be built in the 1860s and 1870s to handle all the processes from fleece to cloth. This came at a time when woollen cloth was back in fashion, with tweeds and the pattern called fancy cloths. Improved ways of reducing old clothing to fibres, the shoddy trade, meant that 40 per cent of fibres were being recycled for use a second time. Since all new wool came from Australia, this represented a saving in costs that helped to make woollen cloths cheaper. Even in 1914, though, most woollen mills were still family firms, employing far fewer people than cotton or worsted mills.

In the case of all three fabrics, as powerlooms became available, the plight of the handloom weavers was grim. The *Leeds Mercury* reported in 1831 that cotton mills in Oldham and Ashton-under-Lyne were hard at work, and those who had formerly woven cotton by hand had to pick up work on fustians or silks when they could. The mechanization of spinning had been serious enough, but had only robbed families of the few shillings earned by it; the head of the house still had his work. When his skill was made obsolete, however, the whole family was plunged into poverty, for there was little work in the mills for men. The agony was drawn out the longest for the woollen weavers, and could be

43 (*Above*) Long fibres, like worsted and flax, were spun on Saxony wheels. These women in Co Down in Ireland have gathered their wheels into one cottage to combine spinning with a chat which took their minds from tired muscles and the long hours they had to work.

45 (*Above*) Nottingham lace was cheaper than pillow lace because part of the process was mechanized. But lace-running, or embroidering, was still done by hand, by women as in the picture, or even by young children. Some started work, full time, at the age of three.

44 (*Left*) Making pillow lace called for good eyesight, attention to detail and infinite patience. Honiton in Devon was the centre for this kind of lace making, where it was done by the wives of fishermen. Lace was used to edge collars and handkerchiefs.

46 (*Right*) Silk doubling. Silk was thrown in mills in Macclesfield and elsewhere. Strands had to be doubled to make them thick enough to weave. Much of the weaving was done in attic workshops in Spitalfields and Bethnal Green in London.

47 The apparatus above the loom is a jacquard. The punched cards were sewn into a loop; each press of the pedal brought the next card round and changed the shed. Every warp thread was weighted with an iron rod.

made worse by other factors. Edwin Butterworth wrote about Rochdale in 1831:

> The woollen manufacturers of this town are in a very depressed state, owing (as some say) to the late advance in the price of wool. The condition of the great mass of the Flannel weavers is wretched in the extreme; from repeated reduction in their wages an able journeyman cannot obtain more than 5 or 6 shillings [25-30p] a week, and this to support a wife and family. The cotton trade here continues tolerably brisk.

Other Textiles

The three types of cloth so far talked of in this chapter — cotton, worsteds and woollens — accounted for the great bulk of fabrics used in the nineteenth century. There has not been room in a book as short as this to describe the different types of cloth made, nor the marked regional specialities that were still woven. The remainder of the chapter must discuss the fabrics less in demand, though a lack of quantity did not necessarily mean they were unimportant.

The linen industry, for example, underwent its own revolution at about the same time as the worsted trade. Once the process of hackling had been mechanized, it took little time to adapt cotton machinery to handle linen, which was very similar in many respects. A shortage of flax grown in England meant that increasing quantities had to be imported from the Baltic countries, but Ireland had a plentiful supply and a lively linen industry developed there from the middle of the eighteenth century.

The canvas side of the linen industry did very well. All coastal and fishing boats needed sails, and steamships carried them too. The finer linens, though, were steadily replaced by cottons as the quality of those improved. Cotton was even used for sewing thread, which had been an important part of the linen industry. By 1900, linen was fast becoming almost a luxury fabric, reserved for dress materials, best tablecloths and similar uses.

Among the former users of linen thread were the lace makers. This domestic industry flourished in many parts of Britain in the eighteenth century, the most famous area being in the villages around Honiton in Devon. Many of the best decorative motifs came from pillow lace makers there, and were used for cuffs, decorating handkerchiefs and table linen, and for enhancing clothes. A number of Midlands men adapted knitting frames to imitate lace making, and Nottingham fast became the centre of factory lace making. Cotton yarn was increasingly used in place of linen, making lace curtains a possibility for most families.

The silk manufacturers were the least interested in the new machines. The popularity of silk materials came from their shine and fine patterns, despite their cost, and mechanization was discouraged by the shortage of raw materials. Some cotton spinning machines were adapted to spin silk waste, which made a

48 This Yorkshire mill was built in 1912 for spinning worsted yarn. It was one of the last to be built before the depression, and its style indicates confidence in the future of the industry.

cheap yarn that could be used to decorate other fabrics. The process of silk throwing could not be greatly improved, other than to make better machines out of iron and drive them with steam power. Following trends in fashion, silk was woven with worsted and cotton yarns to make small flowers, birdseyes or attractive patterns. The apparatus used for this was the jacquard, a French invention that was introduced into Britain about 1830. This was used for all fine yarns if very complicated patterns were being woven. Though at first it was fitted to a handloom, it was operated by punched cards (like computers a century later), and could equally be fitted to a powerloom. A simpler version had existed for some years, and was used to weave a wide variety of geometrical patterns from woollen yarn.

These minority fabrics, providing for specialist or ornamental needs, were an important part of the textile industry. Cottons, worsteds and woollens, however, were the solid base of textiles at this time. The average annual value of all exports in the early 1880s was £234 million. Textiles made up nearly half this figure (46 per cent), and cotton alone accounted for a third of it (32.5 per cent). Few cotton manufacturers seemed alarmed at this time about another profitable export — textile machinery.

7. The Old and the New

The war that started in 1914 has sometimes been called the 'engineers' war', because it was a battle between rival groups of industrialized countries. It lasted four years. During that time, British industries suffered the greatest shake-up since the Industrial Revolution, which was the greater for affecting all industries at the same time. It was inevitable that the older industries should go through a period of upheaval at some time, for they had become increasingly complacent since 1880, as if they felt that the world would go on buying more

50 The depression hit all textile workers but particularly those in the cotton mills. Marches to London and demonstrations could not halt the decline in the industry.

British goods each year to the end of time without anybody having to think about it.

Signs of a change had been clear for some years. Germany, the United States, France and Japan were the leaders among many countries that had undergone their own industrial revolutions in the second half of the nineteenth century. Their firms had more modern machinery and production methods than most British companies because they had developed so much later, and this meant they could produce the same goods at less cost. In addition several cotton using nations had over the years been slowly developing their own factories. A time when British exporters faced stiffer competition was bound to come, and the war served to accelerate the process, crowding most of the changes into the war years, though it was some years later before the full extent of the changes began to be realized.

Cotton Crash

The cotton manufacturers were the hardest hit. They were utterly dependent on imported raw cotton, and this was in short supply during the war because space in merchant ships was reserved for food and other essential supplies. It was the same with exports — cotton cloth for India was considered less urgent than tanks for the troops. Indians, and all the other customers of British

51 Automatic looms were used for cotton, worsted, woollen and linen goods. They stopped if the weft broke, or the shuttle needed a new bobbin. One woman supervised several looms. The noise was such that weavers had to lip-read each other.

cottons, could not manage without it for an indefinite amount of time, and had to find alternative supplies. Many new cotton mills were built in India, filled with machinery copied from the English machines bought earlier. Japanese manufacturers did the same, so rapidly that they were exporting cotton cloth to neighbouring countries by 1918. The results of these changes are illustrated by the figures in the following table:

cotton cloth, in millions of square metres		
	produced	exported
1912	6,731	5,780
1924	5,039	3,715
1930	2,776	2,013
1935	2,831	1,629
1937	3,585	1,672

Cotton manufacturers thought that trade would go back to normal within a few years of the end of the war. However, though the world consumption of

52 Many textiles were woven for making into clothes, and the mass-production of clothes began to become a factory trade at the end of the nineteenth century. These girls are using rubberized cloth to make macintoshes.

raw cotton was back to pre-war levels by 1925, the amount used in Lancashire was not. Instead it continued to fall during the depression years which followed. The output of yarns was lower than at any time since the cotton famine, and more cloth had been woven in the 1850s than was in the 1930s. India had been Lancashire's best customer — nearly all the 2,641 million square metres of cloth she bought in 1914 had come from Britain. Indian mills were built up so quickly that only 639 million square metres were needed in 1937, of which 279 million were bought from Britain and 349 million from Japan. This was an annual loss of a staggering 2,257 million square metres of cloth a year.

Figures of such magnitude are hard to comprehend, but perhaps indicate something of the disaster that fell on Lancashire. The other cotton producing areas were also affected but most had alternative employment available. South Lancashire and north Cheshire, though, were totally committed to cotton, and losses in trade of these proportions were disastrous. In 1924, there were about 3,000 firms in the area, each specializing in one of the four activities of the industry — spinning, weaving, finishing or merchanting. All mills were on short-time working then, for that had been the normal course of action whenever trade fell. When it became obvious that this was not a short-lived decline in trade, other measures were tried, such as agreements between firms to hold down prices or to limit output. Nothing helped. The export balloon had burst, and there was too little profitable work to go round all the mills and workers. Many mills went bankrupt, others were bought up and closed. Either way, many thousands of people lost their jobs, machine minders and managers alike. The numbers employed in the industry fell by 43 per cent between 1923 and 1938. The misery of those unemployed for several years was severe, a warning of the human dangers of allowing an area to be dependent on only one industry. The dole was chilly comfort to those whose jobs had died on them.

Those still employed in the cotton mills had harder work to do. A weaver, whose experience of textile mills had started in 1904 at the age of twelve, described conditions in 1922:

Work inside the factory is much harder than it used to be owing to the great speeding up of the machinery. The toil is now almost ceaseless; the machinery demands constant attention. Thirty years ago this was not the case; the machinery ran very much slower and the operatives had a little leisure during working hours, but all this has been abolished . . . For 48 hours a week year in and year out one is expected to keep up to the great machine monsters. While the machinery runs the workers must stand; it cares nothing for fatigue or weakness or worry, and must not be interfered with by human pain or woe.

Were it not for its effect upon human beings, a textile mill would be a

53 Rayon, like the later synthetic fibres, was handled on traditional textile machinery, such as this ring spinning frame.

splendid monument to man's skill ... One looks with wonder at the automatic looms of today which stop just at the right moment and dispose of the empty shuttle, pick up a full one and restart as though possessed of magic power. One is inclined to think 'what a boon to the worker', but this is not the case, because a weaver of ordinary looms tends two, but an automatic weaver tends four with very little difference in wages.

Valuable Home Market

The worsted and woollen industries were also hit hard after the war, for similar reasons. The war had been a busy time for woollen firms as they produced uniform cloths by the mile, and worsted firms had also had plenty of work. Both were helped by being able to use a home-produced raw material. After the war, exports dwindled for the same reasons as the cotton firms'. Customers in European countries had found alternative suppliers during the war, though trade with Japan and China increased until 1924, when exports fell further

54 There has not been room in this book to discuss many of the less obvious kinds of textile manufacture. This machine, a form of carding engine called a devil, is preparing horse hair for stuffing chairs and sofas.

while the depression lasted. This brought some bankruptcies, redundancy and short-time working in Yorkshire mills but not on the same scale as in Lancashire. The numbers employed in woollen and worsted mills fell by 32 per cent between 1923 and 1938. About half the cloths made from wool had always been sold inside Britain and, though even this declined during the worst years of the depression (1929-33), much cloth was still required.

The target for all three industries was to find as much work as possible, even if it meant trying some unusual ways. In 1929, for example, many Lancashire mills abandoned their usual mistrust of others to form the Lancashire Cotton Corporation. This soon owned 140 spinning mills, of which half were scrapped, but still they could not find enough work for the people employed in the rest. Cotton weaving mills tried to vary their goods by switching to rayon fabrics (*see later*) or cotton/rayon blends. This forced spinning mills to find new markets, and they sold more to Midlands hosiery firms and to the rubber industry for reinforcing tyres. Finally the industry had to accept government direction: the Cotton Industry Reorganization Act, 1936, set up a board to buy up and scrap surplus mills and machinery. This was the final recognition that the days of Britain supplying the world with cotton were gone. As with the woollen industry in 1700, however, the loss of half its trade did not mean that the cotton industry was dead. After 1936, there was still a permanent need for cotton bed 'linen', shirts, blouses and many other items, and sales in European countries rose a little until the Second World War (1939-45) put an end to that again. Woollen and worsted firms similarly accepted mergers, takeovers and the closure of surplus mills. They too had resolved most of their immediate problems by 1939, though the uncertain state of trade discouraged them from replacing old machinery with new.

The linen industry continued its slow decline in these years, increasingly producing near-luxury goods. The decline in sailing ships cut out much of the demand for canvas, and most of that still made was of cotton fibre anyway because it was so much cheaper. The silk industry, however, was faced with unique difficulties by the development of the first successful synthetic fibre: rayon, or artificial silk.

Man-made Fibre

Several man-made fibres had been tried in the nineteenth century in different parts of Europe but all had proved too expensive. In 1892, Charles Cross and Edward Bevan found a cheap way of making a fibre by treating wood pulp with different chemicals. The cellulose obtained was drawn out into almost endless and very fine filaments. These were shiny, like silk, and could be lightly spun together in much the same way that silk was thrown. Calling it artificial silk was a fair description of its properties. An old established silk firm thought so — Samuel Courtaulds bought the rights to manufacture rayon, and had perfected the necessary techniques in time to produce useful quantities during the First World War. A finer filament was made by a different process, using cellulose acetate, and this was manufactured by British Celanese after 1918.

Much of the new yarn was used to make silky cloths at a price that far more people could afford than if it had been pure silk. About 70% of 'silk' dresses were made of rayon in 1939, and filament yarn was increasingly used in the years between the wars for coat and suit linings because it slid so easily over other fabrics. Curtains and upholstery fabrics were also made of rayon, or contained some to give a contrast with the other fibres used. Filament yarn was also used to make cords for reinforcing car tyres. It was much stronger than cotton, which meant that less rubber was needed. Apart from this direct competition with cotton, the popularity of rayon did not seriously upset any of the natural fibre manufacturers. Artificial silk carved a new market for itself by providing silky goods at much lower prices than real silk, though that was still available for those who wished to pay for it. Problems about dyeing the new fibre were mostly overcome by 1920, for experience had shown that it

81

dyed much like cotton. The figures in the following table show the steadily increasing popularity of goods made from rayon filament yarn.

Production of rayon, in thousands of tonnes		
	filament yarn	staple fibre
1934	349	23
1935	420	63
1936	454	136
1940	521	612

Towards the end of the First World War, when supplies of good wool were running low, combers began to use waste rayon to eke it out. The waste was made up of short lengths of filament, similar to long wool fibres. Experience learned in the war showed that wool/rayon blends might have some advantages over all-wool cloths, so after 1918 Courtaulds began producing rayon suitable for woollen processing. The filament was chopped into short lengths, and made to match the natural fibres as accurately as possible. This was called staple fibre (the trade name was Fibro), and in the 1920s was tried by the cotton manufacturers more than any others — they had a greater need to find something new. All kinds of novelty cloths were made but they were expensive, and the fashion was quickly killed by the depression. It had served, though, to introduce people to synthetic fibres. In the 1930s, manufacturers took greater care in blending different fibres, and mixture cloths became a permanent part of textiles production. The figures in the table above indicate the rapid growth of this side of rayon production. By 1940, it was being blended with cotton for hosiery, with silk for bedspreads and underwear, with linen for tablecloths and with wool for blankets, carpets, upholstery and overcoat cloths.

While the public were beginning to accept rayon, new and better synthetic fibres were being developed. Nylon was one, discovered by Wallace Carothers in America in 1937. This could be spun finer than rayon, so much so that a new set of sizes, called the denier scale, had to be devised to measure the thickness of nylon yarns. Nylon was immediately popular when it reached Britain in 1939 — 64 million pairs of stockings were sold at £1 a pair. Another new fibre, terylene, was developed in 1941 by J R Whinfield and J T Dickson. Both nylon and terylene were immediately diverted to war needs, for parachutes and glider ropes, and their development for peacetime use belongs to the next chapter.

8. Drip Dry and Throw Away

Synthetic Fibres

In 1940, Courtaulds and ICI jointly formed British Nylon Spinners, and developed factories at Coventry and Stowmarket to make goods for the war effort. The varied uses to which nylon could be put indicated that it would become popular faster than rayon had, so British Nylon Spinners opened the largest nylon factory in Europe in 1948, at Pontypool in Monmouthshire. Others were built at Doncaster and Gloucester.

Nylon was made from polymer chips, which were melted and extruded through spinnerets — rather like miniature watering cans. The nylon hardened as it cooled, and was then stretched to four times its original length, which made it strong, white and shiny. Like other synthetic fibres, it could be used as filament yarn, or chopped into short lengths and used as staple fibre. Wartime clothes rationing ended in 1949, and the public began to see the wide range of

55 Synthetic fibres being 'spun', or rather stretched to make them fine and glossy.

fabrics that nylon could make. Stockings had been known before the war and soon became available again, joined by underwear, nightwear, dresses, socks, knitting yarn, knitted goods and many more. Customers soon found that nylon goods not only looked and felt good but that they lasted well too. Moths could not eat nylon as they did wool. There were many industrial uses for it too — for tarpaulins, safety belts, overalls, yacht sails and so on.

Terylene, a polyester fibre, was developed by ICI at about the same time. The company built terylene factories at Wilton in Yorkshire and Kilroot in Ireland. (The terylene factories, British Nylon Spinners and ICI's other interests in textiles were merged together as ICI Fibres in 1965.) Terylene was made in much the same way as nylon. It had most of the advantages of the latter, and some others too. It stayed white longer, for example, before beginning to yellow with age. This made it popular for net curtains in preference to cotton, for it washed much more easily. Also, terylene was resistant to creasing and stretching; alternatively it could be made to have permanent creases. Pleats in shirts and knife-edge trouser creases could now be held in clothes by making them out of a blend of fibres, one of which was a polyester.

ICI, Courtaulds, Du Ponts and several other firms spent vast sums of money developing new chemical fibres in the 1950s and 1960s, based on polyester, acetate, polypropylene, polyurethane and others. Only a few of the fibres discovered were in fact produced commercially because of the astronomic costs of development. Many that were reached the public under a bewildering array of trade names, which made it hard to know what to expect of the material or how to clean it. Cotton and wool were well understood, but what about Orlon, Courtelle, Acrilan, Celon, Evlan, Chatillon, Isovyl, Lycra, Lancola, Tendrelle . . .? Gradually, the public learned how to treat the new fibres, and came to like them, especially when fabrics like Crimplene appeared, which combined the characteristics of different synthetic fibres.

The result of this rapid development of new fibres was a revolution in the way people dressed, and in the way they furnished their homes. The new fibres, either on their own or blended with natural fibres, opened up vast possibilities. The synthetics could be machine washed, they dried quickly and needed little or no ironing. They lasted well, and were cheap enough for everyone to be able to be fashionable. As the prices of raw cotton and wool rose, synthetic fibres became a better buy than ever, until the price of oil, the most common raw material for plastics, rose sharply in 1973. Man-made fibres also made new effects possible, by blending fibres to give different textures or variations in colour because one would take a dye more than another. Above all, synthetics were convenient, making it much easier for married women to go out to work and still run a home.

The changes in women's dress as a result of the new fibres was quite remarkable, but for men it was startling. One of the difficulties that rayon had

56 The factories making synthetic fibres were very different from the nineteenth-century mills. Most of the machines at this nylon factory at Pontypool are housed in single storey workshops, making it easier to transport materials from one process to the next.

had to contend with was that men were reluctant to change from the drab colours and traditional look of their clothes. Within a few years of man-made fibres being readily available, however, men could be seen wearing shirts in all colours of the rainbow, and pin-striped suits gave way to much brighter and more varied clothes. The rediscovery of colour spread to the home, contrasting with the lifeless colours that had necessarily marked the depression and war years. Synthetic fibres gave carpets, curtains and upholstery a new look, for they were stronger than the natural fibres and could be made much lighter. Alternatively, traditional designs could be made from cheaper materials and brought within the reach of a wider public.

Natural Fibres

The sudden popularity of the new fibres was bound to cause problems for the natural fibre manufacturers. Cotton firms, still reeling from the decimation of the industry after 1920, now faced the loss of trade in cloths for shirts, dresses, sheets and similar goods. Some changed to weaving the new yarns, others to blends, while there was still sufficient demand for cotton to keep some manufacturers in business. Woollen and worsted manufacturers, blanket makers and carpet firms all had to come to terms with the public's preference for the new fibres though, as with silk, there was always a significant minority of people prepared to pay extra for goods made entirely of natural fibre. Most firms were taken by surprise in the 1950s, and had no answer to give to the obvious advantages of synthetics. They began to fight back in the 1960s with research, devising processes that would give to natural fibres the advantages people saw in synthetics — making woollens machine-washable, for instance.

They were helped by a change in public attitude. People began to realize that synthetics were marvellous for some things but not for everything. A polyester blanket was not as warm as a wool one, and a worsted suit had a 'quality' look about it that no stretch fabric with permanent creases could attain. Many people found nylon unpleasant to wear next to the skin, and it produced static electricity, which attracted dirt. The new fabrics could not be starched, and could not be made to look crisp. So towards the end of the 1960s, people began to turn more and more to blends which combined the best characteristics of both natural and synthetic fibres. The following table concerns the fabrics that people liked for sheets, but it illustrates the general change in the kinds of textiles people wanted.

Approximate percentage preferences for sheet fabrics					
	flat cotton	cotton flannel-lette	linen	nylon	polyester/cotton
1963	50	50	slight	—	—
1968	40	40	slight	20	—
1975*	33	33	slight	4	30
*estimate					

Re-equipment

The natural fibre users were all old, established industries. The shock of synthetics soon wore off, and individual firms set about making themselves more efficient and better able to cope with future developments. Many firms, for example, were still using machinery made 80 or 100 years before. It still worked as well as ever, for nineteenth-century engineers built things to last, but it was slow and becoming harder to repair as spares became difficult to find.

A massive modernization programme began in the 1950s to make the mills competitive in the modern world. Much of the machinery for this had to be imported, for the loom makers in Germany and Switzerland were far ahead of their English counterparts. Looms using the flying shuttle were still the most popular, and ingenious attachments were designed, capable of being fitted to any loom, which would automatically wind the bobbins, fit them in the shuttles and re-start the loom. A Chorley mill equipped with these employed 15 people to supervise 180 fully automatic looms.

Some loom designers tried new ideas. A popular Swiss loom simply used the shuttle as a carrier to draw the yarn from one side to the other. This was very fast, and was capable of weaving 25cm of worsted in a minute. Rapier looms replaced the shuttle with a long arm which passed the yarn through the shed, and looms using jets of air or water were also installed. Much spinning machinery had to be imported too, though high-class finishing machines continued to be made in Britain.

Most of the new machines came complete with electric motors. This was only to be expected in the 1950s, but it was one more reason to replace the mills' existing sources of power with electricity. A substantial number of mills had until then been content with their steam engines, and there was plenty of life left in them. Most, however, were scrapped in the 1950s, though a few were left where they lay because no one could bear to break them up. Some engines had already been adapted to generate electricity, but most firms were persuaded to abandon their obsolete plant and rely on the local electricity board.

Mills with water wheels were forced to change over because of the high price of timber and the scarcity of skilled wheelwrights. A few far-sighted managers installed turbines instead, run from the existing mill-pond, and this was a help during periodic power crises. All this re-equipment cost money, much of which

57 Many of the textile mills were still using late nineteenth-century machinery in the 1950s. It was slow but functioned perfectly well, and was better suited to making short lengths of a pattern.

58 Where do 'textiles' end and something else begin? Redundant ring spinning frames have here been adapted to spin pipe cleaners from wire and waste nylon fibres.

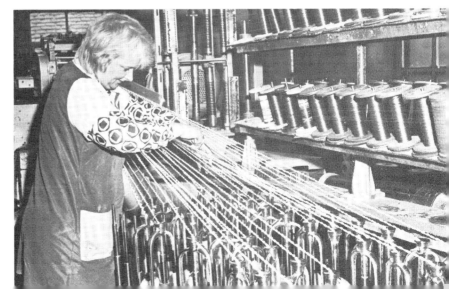

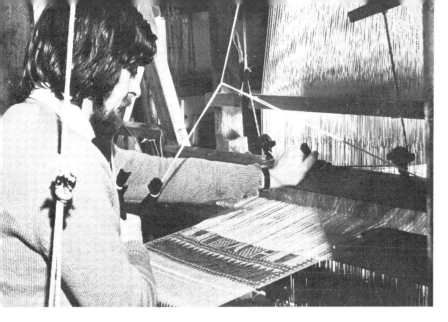

59 Some textiles are deliberately made on old machinery because it is of interest to visitors, or because it is an economical way to make short lengths of very individual designs.

was accumulated by firms taking over others and forming giant combines. This was particularly so in the cotton and worsted industries. What with electric motors, new machinery and some experience of blending natural and synthetic fibres, those firms still left in 1970 felt ready to face anything.

Non-Woven Fabrics

Several firms had started experimenting with new ways of making textiles in the 1960s, and by 1970 they were producing significant amounts of non-woven fabrics. As with every new textile described in this book (and with others omitted for lack of space), the firms producing non-woven fabrics began by trying to make cheap goods to replace the ones made by other processes. There were two purposes for non-wovens; disposable goods intended to be thrown away after being used a few times or perhaps only once, and more durable products. Among disposables were nappies and nappy liners, protective clothing for people working in messy, infectious or contaminated conditions, sheets for hospitals and table 'linen' for hotels. There was also a wide variety of dusters and wiping cloths, since the rags that people would normally have used were no longer absorbent if they were made of fibres like nylon. The durable goods included filters for air conditioning and purifying liquids, interlinings for clothes, and bases and backing for carpets, strippable wallpapers, shoe linings, adhesive tapes and many similar uses.

Three separate ways of making non-wovens were developed, each producing a fabric suitable for a different purpose. The most common way was called dry-laid, and it made use of adapted carding machines from the natural fibre users. Rayon staple was the usual fibre, with some nylon and polyester too, but no special fibres were needed. The fibres were carded into a thin film, which was coated with adhesive by rollers, sprays or in other ways. The thickness of the fabric could be altered to suit its intended use, and several layers could be laminated together (like plywood). The adhesive could be used to dye the fabric, or to fill it with disinfectant, polish or any other special additive. Nearly all disposable goods were dry-laid, and many others also.

The other principal method was to have the fabric spun-bonded, that is the filaments were extruded from the spinnerets straight into a fabric. This more complex method made a cloth that was lighter yet just as strong. It therefore tended to be used for more durable purposes, such as carpet backing, upholstery and making shoes.

The third method was called wet-laid, and more logically forms part of the paper industry than of textiles. Adapted paper-making machinery was used, and the fibres strained from a liquid as they moved through the machine. The resulting product was used for tea-bags, and tried without much success for disposable dresses.

Non-woven fabrics first became significant in Sweden during the Second World War. Normal supplies of raw materials were cut off, and alternatives had to be found out of native products. By 1972, 99 per cent of all Swedish babies were wearing disposable, non-woven nappies. At that time only 8 per cent of British babies were using them, but the proportion was increasing at the expense of firms making the traditional cotton nappies. It was the same with many other non-woven products, which could be produced more cheaply than the goods they replaced. This was clearly the case with dusters and wiping cloths, which had the added advantage that they would cut easily into squares without fraying at the edges. The use of disposable non-wovens for clothing was much slower to develop, for it took almost as long (and so cost as much) to tailor a boiler suit from non-woven as from woven materials. If the making up could be automated, the manufacturers of non-wovens would be set for further expansion. As it was, the pace of technical development in the 1970s closely resembled the cotton industry of the 1760s:

A noticeable feature when considering future developments is the almost complete lack of new machinery. It would still seem to be up to the efforts of individual manufacturers to develop his own plant to achieve higher productivity, via greater efficiency, lower manpower, higher speeds and less waste.

Future Trends

Oddly enough, it was during the period that non-wovens were being developed that tourism hit textiles production. The increasing mobility of people on holiday made it possible as well as interesting for them to visit mills and workshops in out-of-the-way places. Handloom weavers in the Hebrides were a popular port of call as were water powered mills in Wales. The contribution made by such manufacturers to the total textile output was infinitesimal, but visitors remembered the individualistic patterns they had seen, and realized that mass production may have kept prices down, but that it also left everyone with much the same kind of patterns, colours and fabrics. In this way, some manufacturers were encouraged to make traditional patterns, and to design new ones that were unique. Goods made by traditional means were expensive but people were prepared to pay more for some of the fabrics they used. The interest in 'tie and dye' in the home was another example of people seeking something different.

It is perhaps foolhardy to speculate on the future development of the textile industry. Much will obviously depend on the relative prices of raw materials, since every branch of the industry is dependent on imports for at least part of its needs. The development of cost-reducing techniques in one branch of the industry will clearly give that an advantage over the others.

Fashion plays an important part in the fabrics used for clothes, and to a lesser extent for furnishings, though the industrial use of textiles is largely determined by value for money compared with alternative goods. Some forecasters see people in the future having a small range of clothes, probably made of mainly natural fibres, kept for repeated use, and a larger selection of disposable garments to ring the changes. The pace of scientific and technical change is rapid, and is likely to produce some interesting results when it is harnessed to a tradition of textile manufacture covering so many centuries.

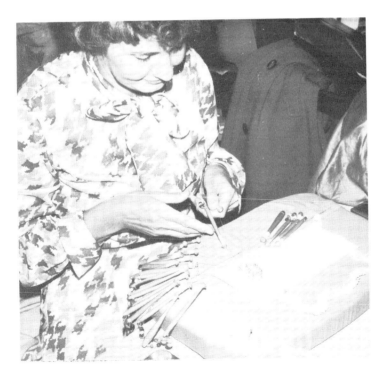

60 Some forms of textile manufacture have become leisure activities. This lady had spent a term learning the difficult art of pillow lace before making this edging.

Further Information

There are many books in print about textiles, most of them very detailed. Among the shorter ones are titles in Longmans Then and There series, such as *Wool Merchants of the Fifteenth Century*, and *A Border Woollen Town in the Industrial Revolution*. For synthetics, there is G.S. Ranshaw, *The Story of Rayon* (Burke Publishing Co, 1945). There is also Marjorie Wilkerson's *Clothes* in the Batsford Past-into-Present Series.

Among more weighty recent books are E. Lipson, *A Short History of Wool and its Manufacture* (Heinemann, 1953), H. Heaton, *The Yorkshire Woollen and Worsted Industries* (Oxford, 1965), J.G. Jenkins, *The Wool Textile Industry in Great Britain* (Routledge & Kegan Paul, 1972) and *The Welsh Woollen Industry* (National Museum of Wales, 1969), A. Plummer and R.E. Early, *The Blanket Makers* (Routledge & Kegan Paul, 1969), J. de L. Mann, *The Cloth Industry in the West of England, from 1640 to 1880* (Oxford, 1971) and A.P. Wadsworth and J. de L. Mann, *The Cotton Trade and Industrial Lancashire 1600 – 1780* (Manchester University Press, 1965); also W. English, *The Textile Industry* (Longman, 1970). W.G. Rimmer, *Marshalls of Leeds, Flax-spinners* (Cambridge, 1960) and E.M. Sigsworth, *Black Dyke Mills* (Liverpool University Press, 1958) describe individual firms. These are all very detailed and should be dipped into rather than read.

Books written in the nineteenth century can still be interesting, especially in small doses. A number have been reprinted in recent years, such as E. Baines, *The Woollen Manufacture of England* (1858), Felkin's *History of the Machine-wrought Hosiery and Lace Manufacturers* and G. Henson, *History of the Frame-work Knitters* (1831). Local books can often provide information about domestic industry, such as Arthur Young's *Tours* and J. Aikin, *A Description of the Country from Thirty to Forty Miles Around Manchester* (1795). F.M. Eden, *The State of the Poor* (1797) has details of domestic industry in many parts of Britain. V.E. Chancellor, *Master and Artisan in Victorian England* (Evelyn, Adams & Mackay, 1969) contains the diary of an employer (William Andrews) and the autobiography of a handloom ribbon weaver (Joseph Gutteridge), which together show the difficulties of the putting-out system. T. Steel, *The Life and Death of St Kilda* (National Trust for Scotland, 1965) is a recent book that describes the bleak background of the island tweed weavers.

Information about textile machinery can be found in *Textiles* (HMSO, 1970) and in greater detail in T.K. Derry and T.I. Williams, *A Short History of Technology* (Oxford, 1960). Most museums in areas that had a specialist

91

textile industry have collected some tools or machines connected with it, and the Science Museum in London has a small display about the major textile industries. There is, however, no national textile museum. Among museums with collections of more than local interest are Old House Museum, Bakewell, Derbyshire; Lewis Museum of Textile Machinery, Blackburn, the Tonge Moor Textile Machinery Museum, Bolton, and Helmshore Museum, all in Lancashire. These are mainly concerned with cotton, and the Bradford Industrial Museum in Yorkshire keeps a range of worsted machinery in working order. There is no comprehensive woollen museum, but a complete woollen mill has been re-erected at the Welsh Folk Museum at St Fagans, Cardiff, and handloom weaver's cottages have been restored at Kilbarchan, Renfrewshire, and Golcar, Yorkshire. All these three show the various processes, and the Colne Valley Museum at Golcar allows visitors to operate a handloom, and so form some idea of the work involved. Linen and silk looms can be seen in the Bridewell Museum, Norwich, a display of lace making methods at Nottingham Industrial Museum, and of pillow lace at Honiton Museum, Devon. The Irish linen industry is recorded in the Ulster Museum and Ulster Folk Museum, in Belfast. As textiles have been made everywhere, weavers' cottages and mills can be found in all counties or see Hugh Bodey's *Discovering Industrial History and Archaeology* (Shire, 1975).

Among interesting novels based on textiles are C. Harnett, *The Woolpack* (Puffin, 1961) and Phyllis Bentley, *The Adventures of Tom Leigh*, *Take Courage*, *Inheritance*, *The Rise of Henry Morcar* and *A Man of His Time*.

Glossary

Bleach	To make white.
Broadcloth	Cloth woven on a broad loom of four quarters or more. More particularly, a high quality plain weave woollen cloth, mostly made in the West Country.
Calico	The name given to cotton cloth when it was first brought to Britain by the East India Company.
Canvas	A coarse linen cloth, used for ship and windmill sails, tarpaulins, tents and similar heavy duty purposes.
Carding	The process of breaking down locks of wool into a sliver of fibres suitable for spinning. (The sliver is also called a carding.)
Combing	The process of removing short fibres from the long ones used for worsted spinning, and making the long ones parallel ready for spinning.
Cropping	Shearing surplus fibres from woollen cloth after it has been raised.
Distaff	A stick, sometimes forked, to hold carded wool in a convenient place for hand spinning.
Drop spindle	A short stick used by hand spinners to stretch fibre and spin it into yarn.
Filament yarn	Yarn made by lightly twisting long, fine strands of silk or synthetic fibre, so that the yarn keeps the natural gloss of the fibre.
Finishing	All the processes that follow weaving and make cloth ready for the customer, such as dyeing, cropping, bleaching or pressing.
Flannel	A thin woollen cloth that has been heavily fulled.
Frame knitting	Knitting on a stocking frame, invented in the sixteenth century.
Frame loom	A handloom that came into general use in the Middle Ages, and was based on a substantial wooden frame (*see illustration* **39**).
Fuller's earth	A natural clay, used for washing grease from woollen cloth.
Fulling	The process of felting woollen cloth by pummelling it in water.
Fustian	A mixture cloth, commonly of a linen warp and cotton weft, used for overcoats and jackets.
Great wheel	The first kind of spinning wheel to be in general use in Britain.
Heald	A frame, holding a number of eyes through which the warp threads were passed in a handloom. Healds separated the threads to form the shed.
Journeyman	Someone working for a wage.
Kersey	A narrow and rather coarse woollen cloth.
Mordant	A chemical that must be applied to a cloth before it will take a dye.
Narrow cloth	Three quarters wide — the widest that one man could weave unaided unless he had fitted a flying shuttle apparatus to his handloom.
New draperies	Mixture cloths of a worsted warp and woollen weft, which became popular in the sixteenth century.

Noils	The short fibres combed out from wool in preparation for spinning the long fibres into worsted yarn.
Non-wovens	Cloth made by processes other than spinning and weaving.
Piecening	Joining cardings together.
Quarter	Nine inches (22.8 cm), the basic unit of measurement in cloth.
Raising	Fluffing up the fibres of fulled cloth so that they can be cropped.
Ring spinning	A method introduced from America in the nineteenth century, which replaced the mule in many cotton mills.
Saxony (or Scots) wheel	An ingenious spinning wheel, treadle operated, and especially suitable for spinning long fibres such as worsted and linen.
Scribbling	A machine process, used to prepare fibres for carding.
Shalloon	A lightweight worsted cloth, used for dress fabrics and coat linings.
Shed	The gap made between warp threads to allow the shuttle to be passed from side to side.
Shoddy	Reclaimed wool fibres, obtained by breaking down knitted garments and tailors' waste.
Staple fibre	Synthetic fibre cut to the same length as natural fibres to permit blending or to copy the appearance of fabrics made from natural fibres.
Teazle	A plant that produces a spiky seed pod, similar to a thistle.
Tenter frame	A long rack on which woollen cloth was stretched to dry after fulling. The cloth was held by tenter hooks.
Throstle	A machine similar to the water frame and used to spin worsted yarn.
Throwing	Loosely twisting silk filaments to make yarn.
Tops	The wool fibres combed for worsted yarn.
Twill	A design made up of diagonal lines.
Warp	The threads that run through the length of a piece of cloth, giving it its strength.
Water frame	Arkwright's spinning machine, driven by water power.
Weaving comb	A hand comb used in prehistoric times to pack weft threads together.
Weft	The threads woven in and out of warp threads, forming the body of the cloth.
Whorl	The weight fastened to the end of a spindle used for hand spinning.
Willeying	The machine process of breaking open tightly compressed fibres before they can be carded.

Index

The numbers in **bold** refer to pages on which illustrations appear.